POINTERS TO THE PAST:

THE HISTORICAL LANDSCAPE OF

HEBDEN TOWNSHIP, UPPER WHARFEDALE

by

Heather M. Beaumont

with members of the Hebden History Group

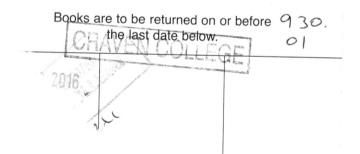

Yorkshire Archaeological Society Occasional Paper No. 5
Series Editor: P R Wilson
Page Layout: J E Wilson

ISBN 1 9035 6455 7

British Library Cataloguing – in Publication data.
A catalogue record for this book is available from the British library.

The Yorkshire Archaeological Society gratefully acknowledges generous grants towards the costs
of publishing this volume from: Local Heritage Initiative, Yorkshire Dales National Park
Authority and Hebden History Group.

Cover illustration: Hebden village and environs from the west.
Field wall (centre foreground) echoes the reverse-S of medieval ploughing. Back Lane lies
between West Field and the planned toft compartment, with Hebden Hall lying to the south and
Town Head farm at the northern limit of the village. The B6265 sweeps diagonally across the
scene, ascending Hebden Bank, with Bank Top farm on the southern side of the road.
Colour plate by kind permission of Alastair Butler, whose generosity is much appreciated.
© *Copyright FOTOAIRE; REF. H6819.*

Back cover illustrations:

1. The village and common arable field as shown on the tithe map (1847), as redrawn by Judith
Joy to include field names and land ownerships.

2. Group members walking the northernmost section of the township boundary, where it follows
the Wharfedale/Nidderdale watershed and is coterminous with the Craven boundary.

Yorkshire Archaeological Society,
Claremont, 23 Clarendon Road, Leeds, LS2 9NZ
(Registered Charity No. 224083)

Printed and bound by:
Smith Settle, Ilkley Road, Otley, West Yorkshire, LS21 3JP

CONTENTS

LIST OF ILLUSTRATIONS

Acknowledgements

This monograph is the outcome of a locality-based study carried out by Hebden residents under the joint leadership of David Joy and the author. In several respects it complements a book written for general readership entitled *Hebden: The History of a Dales Township*, prepared on behalf of the group by David Joy and focusing on the history of the community. Published in 2002, it has been well-received. Individual contributions to the present project are referenced in footnotes. Particular contributions have been made by members of the Hebden History Group[1] (HHG), namely Dorothy Newall and Janet and R. Arthur Stockdale, who created our system for the classification of wall types and carried out much of the recording and interpretation; also Judith Joy whose redrawing of the tithe map, with the inclusion of landholdings and field names, provided an easily accessible and extremely useful reference source. I also wish to thank Hanneke and Edward Dye and Mike Vineall for checking the manuscript: any remaining errors of fact or presentation are my responsibility. I am grateful to all group members for their involvement and enthusiasm and David Joy for encouragement, particularly during the preparation of this work.

Because of the wide scope of our investigations, assistance has been sought - and willingly given - by a number of specialist advisors. We are grateful to Margaret Atherden and Margaret Bastow for carrying out a palynological study; to Mary Atkin, M Phil, for field visits and valuable discussions; Margaret Gelling OBE, DLitt, FBA., for guidance and encouragement; Robert White, Senior Conservation Officer, Yorkshire Dales National Park Authority (YDNPA) for his interest and support, and Angus Winchester PhD., who read an earlier account of our findings and helpfully suggested improvements. Thanks too, to Trevor Croucher (*DataGraphics*) for his skill and care in preparing the maps and other illustrations and for helpful comments; also to Pete and Jill Wilson of the Yorkshire Archaeological Society who have been very supportive while seeing the project through to publication. Other contributions are acknowledged in the relevant footnotes

The Hebden History Group is grateful for financial support for this project, as follows: a Local Heritage Initiative Grant (Local Heritage Initiative is a partnership between the Heritage Lottery Fund, the Nationwide Building Society and the Countryside Agency); The Yorkshire Dales National Park Authority and the Workers Educational Association (WEA, Northern District). These grants have helped to offset the costs involved in documentary research, the preparation and presentation of this work and printing and publication expenses.

Heather M. Beaumont
Brook Street, Hebden.
September 2004.

---

[1] Hebden History Group members contributing to this study: E. A. Bostock, H. Dye, T. Hannam-Whitham, M. Hargraves, P. Hodge, M. Holmes, J. Joy, D. Newall, R. Smith, R.A. & J. Stockdale, M. & M. Vineall, L. Walker.

Summary

Features in the contemporary landscape of Hebden township were examined in an attempt to identify earlier patterns of organisation in the agricultural and built environments. Field observations supported by documentary evidence were used to establish a developmental sequence and likely chronology; interpretation of our findings demanded an holistic view of the evolution of different elements within the township.

In Part 1 we describe the methodology and outcome of a survey of field boundaries, their classification and dating. Most are formed by drystone walls which were categorised according to their composition and construction. Five boundary types were identified, each representing a definable phase in the process of enclosure.

Our survey also revealed a close topographical relationship between those field boundaries judged to be the oldest and routeways which respect, and thus help to define, enclosed compartments, both within and outside the nuclear village (Part 2). This information was used to construct a model of the layout of manorial Hebden (Part 3).

In Part 4 we examine further clues to the way in which elements of the manorial landscape were organised and managed. Then, using the results of our field survey together with documentary evidence (drawn principally from title deeds from the seventeenth and eighteenth centuries and the tithe award and map of the mid-nineteenth century), we trace the development of the agricultural and built landscapes after 1589, when ownership passed from lords of the manor to freeholders.

In conclusion (Part 5) we review significant phases in the evolution of the township, from the establishment of settlement to the layout of the landscape in the mid-nineteenth century. Changes in the physical environment are related to coeval social structures.

Overall, our survey demonstrates the value of an inclusive and integrated approach to the investigation and interpretation of the physical evolution of an individual township and its particular history of ownership and land management.

Introduction

'The English landscape ... is the richest historical record we possess' (W.G. Hoskins).

The quotation comes from Hoskins' introduction to his book entitled *Reading the Landscape*, published in 1955 and generally recognised as the foundation on which the discipline of landscape history has been built.

Today, the concept of 'reading the landscape' implies that, through the development of appropriate methodologies and expertise, it is possible 'to derive a historical narrative from evidence embedded in the visible landscape' (Muir 2000, 7). As recommended by Hoskins, landscape studies have been strengthened by combining empirical observation with documentary research. This approach was also used by Hoskins' contemporary, polymath Arthur Raistrick, who lived in the village of Linton in upper Wharfedale and wrote on many aspects of the history of the region (for bibliographic listing and review see Croucher [1995] and White [2003], respectively). As the subject of landscape history has evolved, it has become increasingly multi-stranded and now incorporates or references many disciplines. This expansion is illustrated by the contents of a review published in 2000 by the Society for Landscape Studies (ed Della Hooke). Additionally, Richard Muir (2000) emphasises the advantages of a non-prescriptive, flexible approach to the design of landscape studies. In general, the multi-disciplinary nature of the subject can be seen in projects that include, for example, environmental and contextural considerations, such as geology and ecology, as well as social and economic factors appertaining locally, regionally or nationally.

Leading exponents in the study of rural settlement and landscape history have similarly called for a widening of the scope of locality-based research. Thus, in the conclusion to their examination of the structural elements of rural settlement, Brian Roberts and Stuart Wrathmell (2002, 2, 192) commend investigations that encompass the entire area of individual townships. These authors also recommend outcomes presented 'in cartographic as well as written form'. Richard Muir (2000,16-17; 2001; 2003, 234) similarly advocates the 'total landscape approach', including the survey of transport networks which 'provide the skeletons of cultural landscapes.' Studies of the process of enclosure, using evidence provided by the landscape itself and backed by documentation, are advocated by Tom Williamson (2003a, 25-6). He encourages analyses of field patterns and the structure of field boundaries, particularly field walls. Serendipitously our project, carried out over the past decade, addresses all of these issues.

The aim of our study *ab initio* was to record features in the contemporary landscape of Hebden in an attempt: (i) to identify earlier patterns of organisation in the agricultural and built environment; (ii) to use field observation supplemented by written evidence to establish a develop-

mental sequence and - if possible - a chronology. Because of the scarcity of documentation relevant to our studies - particularly from the medieval period through to the late seventeenth century - the interpretation of field observations and putative dating rely, to a considerable extent, upon comparison and analogy with the findings of other authors, including those named above. Also helpful have been observations on the layout and features of northern landscapes by Mary Atkin (1982/3; 1985; 1993), Andrew Fleming (1998), Stephen Moorhouse (2003) and Robert White (2002), together with the document-based studies of rural life and landscape, and the management of upland pastoral economies, carried out by Angus Winchester (1987; 2000).

Hebden township is located in the Pennine uplands, within the area known as Craven (Figures 1, 2). The latter featured in the Domesday survey (1086) as *Cravescire* and, almost a century later, was renamed as the Wapentake of Staincliffe, representing a unit of regional administration under the Danelaw. It subsequently served as a medieval deanery and an archdeaconry. Wood (1996) suggests that Craven was a 'little British Kingdom'; one of several established after the Roman withdrawal (*c* AD 400). He further postulates that the name derives from *craf*, one of a group of Welsh words implying scraped or scratched land - a possible reference to the limestone scars and pavements that typify the area. Attractive though this interpretation appears, Professor R. Coates (*pers comm*) advises that it awaits confirmation by further etymological study.[2]

Modern Hebden lies within the ecclesiastical parish of Linton, together with the townships of Linton, Grassington and Threshfield. Townships, as defined by Roberts and Wrathmell (2002, 2), are 'ancient secular units of settlement and community', distinguishable from ecclesiastical and civil parishes. However, in the pre-Conquest period, the townships listed above formed part of an Anglo-Saxon estate and parish centred on Burnsall (Ellis 1875/6, 388-89), (Fig 3). Stone sculptures dating from the tenth century and found in and around the church include three cross-heads and decorated shafts showing an intermingling of Anglo-Saxon and Scandinavian design; also Norse hog-back grave covers. It is likely that Linton parish was 'taken out' of the pre-Conquest parish of Burnsall - an instance of ecclesiastical reorganisation that took place generally during the twelfth century (Winchester 1987, 24). One aspect of parochial organisation outlived this reordering, however: from 1294 to 1579 lords of Hebden were patrons of one mediety of the church in Burnsall.

At the time of the Domesday survey the adjacent landholdings of Osbern de Arches (*ie* Burnsall, Hebden and part of Thorpe) and Gamelbarn (*ie* Linton, Threshfield

---

[2] We are indebted to Professor Richard Coates for his opinion.

and another part of Thorpe) extended across the Wharfe, from watershed to watershed with continuity of cross-river boundaries that survive or can be traced. By 1124 the de Arches lands had been absorbed into the large Honour of Mowbray and sometime between 1138 and 1186 the manor of Hebden was granted by Roger de Mowbray to 'Uctred, son of Dolphin'. By this time a riverine boundary had been established (Beaumont *et al* 2004, 69-70, 75-77) marking a late division of pre-Conquest estates and defining the townships of today.[3] The sequence of manorial lords - first Uctred's descendents the de Hebdens (Greenway 1972, 252), then from *c* 1416 the Tempests of Bracewell,[4,5] - can be followed up to 1589, when the mortgaged manor of Hebden passed into the hands of three freeholders.[6] They adopted the role of trust lords of the manor, exercising the functions and powers of a manorial lord within the community (Raistrick 1971, 41-45). Subsequently the number of freeholders increased, bringing changes in patterns of land-ownership and management.

The character of the contemporary village and its upland setting are illustrated in aerial photographs (*eg* Figs 1, 26). Most buildings within the nuclear village lie to the west of Hebden Beck which flows along a steep-sided, wooded Gill as it approaches the Wharfe. A scattering of farms and outbarns can be seen amongst the fields that surround the village, with several small settlements situated on the moorland fringe. Outcrops of Great Scar Limestone are to be found along the southern edge of the township, near the river. However, as the land rises the soil becomes acidic, overlying shales and sandstones, including the Grassington gritstones (Edwards and Trotter 1954, 17-28, 33). Areas of glacial drift occur in the vicinity of the village. Extending from the River Wharfe (*c* 150m OD) to the Nidderdale watershed (*c* 550m OD) the township boundary (Fig 2) encloses an area of some 1450ha (3,583a), supporting an entirely pastoral agriculture, raising cattle and sheep. The terrain can be divided into three zones. North of the River and surrounding the village nucleus is the area of most intensively managed agricultural land (*c* 365ha or 900a), now meadowland producing silage and hay, as well as pasture of reasonable quality. From an altitude of *c* 300m rising to *c* 360m there is an intermediate zone of *c* 525ha (1,300a) of rough pasture known as Hebden

Moor. Blea Gill marks the boundary between it and Hebden High Moor (also *c* 525ha). Two areas of enclosure are easily distinguished: (i) an irregular patchwork surrounding the nuclear village in which the sizes and shapes of fields show considerable variation; (ii) large rectangular fields on moorland. These are the products of piecemeal enclosure or enclosure by consent, and general or parliamentary enclosure, respectively (Williamson 2000, 2003a; see below and Fig 4). The characterisation of field boundaries in these two zones is the subject of the first part of our study.

Features of the village reflect aspects of the past (Figs 1, 26, 27). Thus, for example, the B6265 Pateley Bridge to Grassington road is the modern representative of a long-established east/west trans-Pennine route. The modern road bridges the beck (GR SE 026631) and transects the village (Beaumont *et al*, 2003). Extending northwards from the site of Hebden Hall, much of the village shows a 'segmental' arrangement, with houses and their associated buildings occupying enclosed, grassed plots. This layout is characteristic of a planned toft compartment within a manorial village (Roberts 1987, 36-7). Furthermore, field boundaries and field markings in the vicinity of the village suggest a pattern of medieval cultivation, underlying and hence preceding the establishment of field boundaries (see below).

Traces of water-powered industrial activity (lead-mining and textile manufacture) can be found within today's pastoral landscape (Joy 1991, 37-59; Gill 1994, 97-114; Hodge 1997). Relics left by operations of the Hebden Moor Mining Company (1846-73) occur north of the village, beyond Hole Bottom hamlet; they follow the course of the beck and spread onto Hebden Moor, around Bolton Gill (Fig 2). In addition, remains originating during the final chapter in the life of the Company can be seen close to the centre of the village from where, between 1873 and 1888, a trial level was driven underground for almost two-and-a-half km: it proved unproductive. A textile mill was built on a site close to the corn mill in 1792 (Fig 27) and reached its height of activity in the mid-nineteenth century.[7] This short-lived industrial phase brought an increase in population and changes in the character of the built environment, prefiguring the village that exists today.

---

[3] Observation by R. Smith (HHG).
[4] Hebden MSS: *Pedigree of the Medieval de Hebdens*, William Hebden of Halifax (1904-73). P*ers comm* Mr. J. Hebden, whose *a*ssistance is gratefully acknowledged.
[5] Tempest MSS: *Tempest Pedigrees*, British Library Tempest MS 40670. Assistance given by Mr. H. Tempest is gratefully acknowledged.
[6] Yorkshire Fines III, *Feet of Fines of the Tudor Period*. Yorks Archaeol Soc Rec Ser (1889*)* **VII**, 121.
[7] Observations on the mills, P T Hodge (HHG).

Part 1. Survey of the agricultural landscape

Our first objective was to record the contemporary agricultural landscape, focussing on the typology of field boundaries, most of which are in the form of drystone walls. Our starting point was the development of a methodology for recording field boundaries and observations were supplemented by information from maps and original documents.

1.1. Classification and recording of field boundaries

The earliest available maps of Hebden date from the mid-nineteenth century. They comprise the tithe award and map of 1846/7 and the parliamentary enclosure award and map of 1857 (hereafter TAM[8] and EAM,[9] respectively), also the first edition Ordnance Survey map, scale 6" to the mile (surveyed 1850-53, published 1857). All provide information about the layout of the agricultural landscape. Both the TAM and the first edition OS map show only those boundaries, situated in the zone between village and moor, that pre-date the Enclosure Act (they are referred to as pre-Enclosure boundaries). The 1910 edition 6" OS map and modern aerial photographs additionally show walls built under the terms of the Enclosure Act on Hebden Moor and Hebden High Moor.[10] The two distinctive forms of enclosure make up a field pattern, most of which remains today and was the starting-point for our field survey (Figure 4). Additional, valuable information about enclosure and landholdings was drawn from the TAM and deeds of title from the seventeenth to mid-nineteenth centuries. Many of the latter are in the collection at the West Yorkshire County Record Office, Registry of Deeds (WYCRO RD). Some of the field names appearing in these documents suggest particular forms of land management.

Our survey was designed to answer the following questions:

(i) Can field boundaries be classified according to their constitution, construction and layout in the landscape? If so:

(ii) Is it possible to determine the sequence in which boundaries were established and walls were built? Further:

(iii) Can a likely chronology of enclosure throughout the township be established?

(iv) Does information about enclosure assist our understanding of past systems of management and the manner in which the agricultural landscape has evolved? If so:

(v) Can this be related to changes in land ownership and/or other factors?

Our first step was to characterise walls constructed under the terms of the Enclosure Act and shown on the EAM, and to distinguish them from preceding boundary types. For the purpose of recording the latter the area surrounding the village was divided into four quadrants, determined by the course of the beck and the B6265 (running roughly north-south and east-west, respectively (Fig 4). Initial observations indicated that there were four types of pre-Enclosure field boundary. The characteristics of each (classified as Groups 1 to 4) are described below and features of interest, together with likely periods of construction and probable role, are discussed. Walls built under the Enclosure Act (Group 5) are described first, since they are easily identified and provide a useful basis for comparison with earlier wall types.

1.2. Parliamentary Enclosure walls (Group 5)

Under the terms of the parliamentary Act (1857), all of Hebden Moor and Hebden High Moor (1075ha, 2660a) were enclosed. The walls were built within a period of 18 months and form a geometrical pattern of predominantly large enclosures implanted on the moorland landscape, characteristically ignoring natural features. They are built of quarried stone that appears roughly coursed and has three rows of regularly spaced through stones that project and pattern the wall surface (Figs 4, 5a, 5b, 7, 8).

Precise specifications for wall construction are not included in the award for Hebden, although the features and measured dimensions of walls shown on the Enclosure Map are similar to those for neighbouring Grassington. Here, walls created by Act of Parliament were to be 34in wide at the base, 6ft high and narrowing (or battered) to a width of 16in (ie 86, 183 and 41cm) 'under the uppermost stone' (ie a course of flat stones underlying the topstones, known as coverstones). There were to be a prescribed number of through stones, placed at regular intervals, in rows 2ft and 4ft (0.61 and 1.22m) from the ground (Raistrick 1978, 8-11). The function of through stones is to confer stability by linking and holding together the two faces of the wall, assisted by coverstones and small stones (fillings) in the wall core. In the Hebden enclosure award, those responsible for the upkeep of specified lengths of walling, who had the right to take stone from the township quarry, were named. Stone was also obtained from small quarries located on moorland, close to where it was required (Fig 9).

1.3. Pre-Enclosure Boundaries

In present-day Hebden most functional field boundaries take the form of drystone walls; there are only a few short stretches of continuous hedgerow. In the northern uplands the earliest boundaries were generally composed of banks topped by dry hedges (ie stakes and brushwood). Winchester (2000, 61-66) presents a body of documentary evidence showing that there was a move, principally during the sixteenth and seventeenth centuries, towards

---

[8] *Hebden Tithe Award and Map* (1846/7): North Yorkshire County Record Office (NYCRO), Northallerton .

[9] *Hebden Moor Enclosure Award and Map*, 1857, parish copy. Transcript, Hebden Enclosure Award (1857) made by A. Raistrick (1942), Ironbridge Gorge Museum Trust (ref. RS 876).

[10] Aerial photographs examined (in addition to those reproduced in this article): (i) Cambridge University Collection: CNM 12 (12.10.80); (ii) BKS Surveys Ltd (Job No. 7406, 12.05.80); copy held by the YDNPA.

greater permanence in field boundaries. This was achieved by the establishment of 'quick' or live hedges, the construction of stone walls, and the re-use or enhancement of embankments. In the contemporary landscape, walls associated with an embankment and/or trees (generally ash) or ancient hawthorns apparently follow the line of boundaries that were originally hedged (Rackham 1993, 188-89). For this reason, information from the first edition OS map - which shows that many of Hebden's field boundaries had more mature trees 150 years ago than they have today - was incorporated into our survey. Boundaries marked by aged thorn trees were also recorded, using evidence from aerial photographs and field survey (Fig 10).

All pre-Enclosure field boundaries within the township were walked and recorded. Each stretch was classified (Groups 1 to 4) and colour-coded on a map template; abutments were also noted. To ensure accuracy and consistency most sites were visited several times and by different recorders. The following criteria were adopted as the basis of our classification.

1.3.1. Boulder walls, relic hedgerows and trees (Group 1)
(Figs 5c, 5d, 10-14)

Many boulder-containing walls are massively built; they are often aligned with a linear feature such as a rocky outcrop or break of slope and generally follow a slightly sinuous course, seeming to reflect 'the lie of the land'. Their constituents and the nature of their construction varies according to the terrain and underlying geology: walls built on a foundation of bedrock gain the biblical advantage of stability. Boulders are utilised in areas where they are easily available. Some of the latter take the form of 'classic' orthostats that have been purposely raised and form a significant structural and visual element, randomly spaced along the wall base. Where lengths of walling have collapsed and been robbed out, the base of the wall is seen to consist of either a single or (more rarely) a double row of raised orthostats, interspersed with blocks of quarried stone or pillow-shaped boulders, laid horizontally along or across the width of the wall; these are referred to as recumbent boulders. There are many instances where walls - constructed 'step-wise' along a contour, embankment or break of slope - have orthostats and/or recumbent boulders which form and support both faces of the wall, yet are visible only from the down-slope.

Dimensions, particularly across the base of boulder walls, are variable, generally around 1.1 - 1.2m, but occasionally reaching 1.5 - 1.8m (3ft 6in - 4ft and 5 - 6ft). Wall height is usually about 1.7 - 1.8m (5ft 6in - 6ft) and may be more when measured from the down-slope. Clearly, when slippage occurs height is reduced and there is spread at the base: Raistrick (1978, 13) describes walls of this type as having the stability of 'a well piled heap of stones'. This implies the use of rounded or partially rounded stones, originating from water-borne or glacial deposits and assembled by field clearance, as found in many of Hebden's walls. The stone in boulder walls is usually ungraded with regard to size, large stones predominating throughout the body of the wall, interspersed with smaller ones filling gaps. Topstones are generally of natural stone; there are instances where they rest on a single layer of flat through

stones that project, generally unilaterally, beyond the wall face. These add to the effectiveness of the barrier in controlling the movement of stock, particularly sheep, or the entry of predators such as wolves. As would be expected, however, there are many instances where the upper parts of boulder walls have been repaired using more recent techniques - such as the grading of stone - which confers an orderly but atypical appearance. Nevertheless, boulder walls are not difficult to identify on the ground, while on aerial photographs their 'organic' course contrasts with the geometrical layout of walls constructed under the Enclosure Act. We found boulder walls bordering routeways and forming boundaries where there are, or have been, differences in land use, namely between pasture and either meadow or arable.

Walls which opportunistically incorporate large random boulders occur in several sites and are included in this category (ie classified as Group 1). These boulders tend to be earth-fast and very large (ie >c 1.5m or 5ft in at least one dimension), often protruding beyond both faces of the wall. Walls of this type notably occur along Scarside, Edgeside and in the vicinity of the township quarry - an area littered with gritstone boulders. Some have been used to form a higgledy-piggledy collection of small closes or animal pens that are difficult to date.

Careful fieldwork enabled us to trace the line of boundaries that have become degraded and gone out of use. Some remain as relic hedgerows consisting of a few ash trees or decrepit hawthorns, generally interspersed with boulders, some in the form of orthostats, and/or rows of tumbled stones. Alternatively they may be reduced to grassed-over embankments or stone foundations. The nature of the association between segments of wall and trees or thorn bushes suggests that upright orthostatic boulders may originally have been recruited, either to stabilise a hedgerow embankment, or to fill gaps between hawthorns as they became 'leggy', thus maintaining stock-proof barriers (Fig 18).

Mapping the distribution of those boundary elements judged to be the oldest (ie relic hedgerows, embankments and boulder walls usually containing some orthostats) unexpectedly and strikingly revealed four large enclosures situated one in each quadrant relating to the nuclear village (Fig 24). Each enclosure is a discrete entity, having a well-defined perimeter. Although different sections of the four perimeter boundaries vary in respect of their composition, the degree of preservation and traceability is good throughout. It is evident that these are primary enclosures since other boundaries, whether inside or outside, abut against them. By analogy with the observations of Mary Atkin, we suggest that these enclosures were created during the medieval period and surrounded four open or common fields: their significance is further examined below and in Parts 3 and 4.

1.3.2. External boundary walls (Group 2)
(Figs 6a, 15, 16)

Although incomplete, two stretches of wall thus classified mark the eastern and western margins of Hebden Moor. Inferences regarding their existence, character and role are drawn from map and documentary information as well as field observations. Confirmation of the creation of a stinted pasture is found in two documents dated 1596/7 and 1600/01 which refer to 'the now inclosed pasture of Hebden' and a dispute concerning the rights of landholders in Hartlington to grazing, and to 'digge turves and get ling', in Hebden pasture.[11]

Map evidence further signifies that parts of the boundary of the stinted pasture are coterminous with sections of the township boundary (ie between Grassington to the west and Hartlington to the east). A stretch of about 2.5km of this wall is preserved on the western side of the township, where it borders part of Hebden Moor, Tinkers' Lane, Mere Lane and Bolton Gill (Figs 2, 15, 16, 39). Features in its construction are unique within Hebden but characteristic of walls enclosing stinted pastures elsewhere, for example in the nearby township of Appletreewick (Mrs. K. Mason, *pers comm*) and also in Swaledale (Fleming 1998, 57-58, Fig 4.2). The Hebden boundary wall is constructed in short lengths (each section *c* 22yds or 1 chain; *ie* 20.5m) delimited by wall heads and punctuated by initials or masons' marks carved into boulders and orthostats in the wall base - features suggesting that responsibility for maintenance was shared. Each section of the wall is further and unequally divided by a third wall head, positioned a gate's width away from a marked division; the significance of this arrangement is not clear. Construction technique is generally crude - in some places the body of the wall is single thickness, with daylight visible between the stones.[12] Quarried material predominates and pieces used in the formation of wall heads are very large and irregular. Stones bearing an incised 'H' are found high on the wall-face, emphasising its role as part of the township boundary, which, on current OS maps, is marked 'foot of wall' on the Hebden side.

Along the eastern township boundary the 1st edition 6" OS map shows a feature marked as 'track of old wall' running between Holes Beck and Blea Beck (now at the head of Grimwith reservoir), (Fig 2). This 'old wall' is thought to represent another section where the boundaries of stinted pasture and township are coterminous. It has largely lost its identity, however, having been incorporated into the pattern of rectangular moorland enclosures created under the Enclosure Acts for both Hebden and Hartlington. Some stretches have been rebuilt; elsewhere it is derelict, reduced to grassed-over foundations or an alignment of boulders. There are no traces of comparable walling beside Blea Beck and we conclude that the northern boundary of the stinted pasture was, effectively, the natural barrier formed by the precipitous sides of Blea Gill and the swiftly running waters of its beck.

1.3.3. Irregular Walls (Group 3)
(Figs 6b, 19, 20)

Walls of this type are irregular in respect of their construction and typically pursue a gently curving and slightly sinuous course. They are generally substantial, *ie* height 1.5 -18m (5 - 6ft); width at the base 0.8 - 0.9m (2ft 6in - 3ft).

In areas where there is evidence of previous cultivation gritstone walls are largely composed of stone derived from field clearance, sometimes with an admixture of quarried stone. Relative proportions of the two types of stone tend to be reversed in walls on the moorland fringe, particularly where stone could be sourced from rocky outcrops or shallow quarries. In both instances the lowermost part of the wall generally consists of several uneven courses of large pieces of stone, some natural and some quarried (approximate dimensions: width 0.8 - 0.9m or 12 - 24in); height and depth 0.2 - 0.3m or 8 -12in). There may be a few - generally small - upright orthostats in the wall base, as well as boulders laid horizontally. The body of the wall typically contains a mix of stone, which is ungraded and uncoursed; there are through stones but these rarely protrude beyond the wall face. Where limestone is used, individual stones are irregularly angular and protuberances and hollows may be approximated, giving a jigsaw like appearance to the wall-face. Topstones are generally of random, natural stone laid transversely across the wall top. Some of them project about 50mm (2in) beyond the face of the wall - another form of deterrent to jumping animals.

This type of walling occurs commonly. Some stretches contribute to the perimeter boundaries of primary enclosures. Others abut onto these boundaries (both internally and externally), which they therefore post-date. Irregular walls erected on embankments or associated with trees or thorns have probably replaced earlier hedgerows, forming property boundaries and field divisions (as shown on the TAM; see below). Dated references to named enclosures (*ie* in title deeds) indicate that this style of walling predominated from *c* 1690 to 1770.

1.3.4. Regular Walls (Group 4)
(Figs 6c, 21)

Walls of this type are few in number. Structurally they closely resemble walls built under the Enclosure Act: the stone is graded (ie the smallest laid closest to the wall-top) and there are regular through stones, which may or may not project. A cover-band is usually present, running flush with well-matched topstones and the upper part of the wall-face. Generally more compact than earlier pre-Enclosure wall types (height 1.4 -1.5m or 4ft 6in - 5ft; width at the base *c* 0.8m or 30in, and width below the topstones 0.3 - 0.4m or 12-15in), these walls generally abut onto Group 3 walls. They often represent adjustments to single boundaries within a farm holding, subdividing already-existing enclosures. Some appear to have replaced hedgerows, being built along an embankment or following an alignment of mature trees. They may predate, or post-date, the EAM. Walls of this type border the turnpike road and are assumed to be contemporary with it (*c* 1760). Comparative mapping (using first and second editions of the 6" OS maps) shows that this form of construction continued in use between 1857 and 1910.

---

[11] Yorkshire Archaeological Society: DD 121/1/4 p; DD 121/1/2 (68). Thanks to Mrs. K. Mason and Dr. A. Winchester for drawing our attention to these documents.
[12] Observation by J. Stockdale (HHG).

1.4. Assessment and interpretation

This system for the classification of field boundaries proved reproducible within the township. The criteria adopted place greatest reliance on the nature of the wall base and use of orthostats and boulders, the character of stone in the main body of the wall, and any special structural features (*eg* protruding through-stones or the frequent occurrence of wall-heads). Also taken into account were the course of walls across the landscape (*ie* whether straight or 'organically linear') and the sequence of construction as judged by wall-to-wall abutments. The latter reveal the sequence in which walls were built and hence provide clues to relative dating. An association with trees, thorn bushes or an embankment is taken to suggest that today's functional boundary replaces an earlier hedge - an inference which accords with the observations of Roberts and Wrathmell (2002, 149-55) in their systematic analysis of field boundaries

We find that typological consistency is maintained, despite the fact that wall-construction and building styles reflect very local variations in geology and topography, as well as the nature and availability of stone. Walls are built pragmatically: the weight of the material predisposes to the use of that which is nearest to hand. Thus wall-lines deviate to incorporate large boulders in areas where they abound. In Hebden, naturally-eroded (recumbent) boulders or blocks of quarried stone are used in tandem with, and outnumber, classic (raised) orthostats.

Stones from field clearance are used in wall-construction, despite their limitations with regard to stability. Repairing a riverside wall composed of rounded, water-worn stones is described by a present-day farmer as 'a nightmare'. Differences in the manner in which stone splits affect the regularity and dimensions of the quarried material. This, in turn, determines the number of 'courses' of stone required to reach the desired height. The progressive refinement of wall-structure must surely also relate to the development of tools and traditional stone-masons' techniques: compare, for example, the crude construction of the boundary wall beside Hebden Moor and Tinkers' Lane with the orderly appearance of walls classified as regular and built 150 - 250 years later. Many variations of style can also be seen in those (Group 4) walls that border the turnpike and are assumed to date from *c* 1760. Their present appearance may reflect differences in style adopted, either by the original wallers, or those responsible for subsequent repairs. As well as pursuing a course that is ruler-straight, walls built under the Enclosure Act adhere to prescribed dimensions, the regular positioning of protruding through stones and the shaping of topstones, all of which confer an orderly appearance.

Typically composed of boulder walls and embanked and relic hedgerows, our findings suggest that the perimeters of Hebden's four primary enclosures represent the first generation of internal boundaries that survive. This conclusion accords with that of Roberts and Wrathmell (2002, 114-17, 132) who suggest that 'ovals' are primary structures enclosing areas of early clearance, 'unconstrained by any pre-existing boundaries'. Features of the boundaries of Hebden's four primary enclosures are illustrated in aerial photographs and maps and described in their ac-

companying legends (Figures 28 and 29, 32 and 33, 36 and 37, 40 and 41; see also Appendices 1-4). The primary enclosures thus defined closely resemble the 'ovals' (400 to 800m in diameter) recorded in Lancashire and Cumbria by Mary Atkin. She established that their perimeter boundaries are characteristically substantial and respected by other boundaries. She also noted that the outer limits of these enclosures often lie close to township boundaries, while routeways generally pass around and outside them. In the region she studied, many such boundaries were in the form of embankments topped by hedgerows and were thought to date from the early post-Conquest period. However, attempted dating depended on Hooper's rule (simplified formula, one indicator species = one century of age), now largely discredited. Nevertheless, the composition and form of hedges 'is not random and can, at least in broad terms, be related to their origins and age' (Williamson 2003a, 26-27).

Our survey has enabled us to define the sequence in which boundaries were established and suggest a likely chronology and relative dating. Clearly, absolute dating cannot be achieved by field observation alone. And although comparative mapping or a reference in a title deed may suggest the date of origin of a particular boundary, precise documentation is required to establish its nature and to show whether the original has survived, or whether what exists today is a replacement.

Using field observation backed by documentation, Arthur Raistrick (1978, 13) ascribed boulder walls in the Yorkshire Dales to the monastic period. The earliest field walls on the North York Moors are similarly reputed to be medieval. Known as head dykes, they separate managed land from less productive moorland and are characterised by upright orthostats in the wall base (Spratt, 1998). As Winchester (2000, 52-55) has shown, head dykes were an integral part of stock management systems in the northern uplands during the late medieval period. They tend to be thought of as a linear frontier or 'tide-mark of enclosure', lying between improved land and grazing grounds on the open moor. However, there are many instances where full protection of the former necessitates the creation of an encircling barrier: for example, where land managed as meadow and/or arable forms an island within the waste, or where the boundary is partially encircled by a drove route.

In a comprehensive survey of landscape evolution on the Cistercian estate or sheep-farm at Royston Grange in Derbyshire wall-types were related to phases of occupation, as revealed by the archaeological record (Hodges 1991; Wildgoose 1991). The results showed that walled boundaries range in date from the second millennium BC (early Bronze Age) to the parliamentary enclosures of the early nineteenth century. Two oval enclosures dated to the Romano-British period were identified. Hour-glass in form and bounded by a double orthostat wall, each is c 0.5 km in diameter; one encloses pasture and the other arable land. In addition, there is a single large enclosure or inpasture for sheep (*c* 1.0 x 0.75 km) bounded by walling of the fourteenth or fifteenth centuries: wall-foundations consist of a single row of 'massive dolomitic boulders' and the upper part of the wall comprises a single thickness of 'rough dolomitic stones'. Although similarities exist, for example in the use and long-term survival of orthostatic boulders in wall foundations, comparable archaeological evidence is lacking for Hebden and walling materials and hence wall-morphology differ. These discrepancies illustrate the difficulty of producing a methodological blueprint for the typology and dating of upland field walls which would be generally or widely applicable.

This situation may change, however, as an outcome of the present study, a survey carried out by Tom Lord (2004) of stone walls in the limestone country around Malham and in Ribblesdale (in the Settle area of Craven) and the overview of northern enclosed landscapes presented by Roberts and Wrathmell (2002, 162-64). Common features emerging from Tom Lord's study and that on Hebden particularly refer to the classification of the first generation of walled boundaries. They include: (i) the presence of orthostatic boulders in the wall base; (ii) a course of unilaterally protruding through stones below the top stones; (iii) similar overall dimensions, and (iv), the fact that the two faces of the wall are only slightly battered upwards from the base, rising to a width of 0.5m (20in). Criteria common to both studies have similarly been employed in the classification of later generations of walling and it may soon be possible to agree a framework for recording field walls that

is applicable within Craven, and possibly elsewhere in the Yorkshire Pennines. On the basis of comparison with the observations of Raistrick (1978; see above) and his own field observations and map evidence, Tom Lord dates orthostatic walls to the thirteenth century. However, this estimate may represent a *terminus ante quem* (*ie* the time at or before which the dating applies).

Studies in Hebden demonstrate clear differences in the typology of walls associated with piecemeal versus parliamentary enclosure. As defined by Williamson (2003a, 16) piecemeal enclosure, or enclosure by consent, was achieved by private agreement, leading to the consolidation of strips and creation of boundaries within the common fields. In addition, the classification and mapping of wall types has enabled us to identify four primary enclosures and has confirmed a topographical association between the perimeters of these primary enclosures and 'old' routeways that pass outside and around them (Figs 24, 25). This association provides a further key to deciphering the historical landscape of Hebden and is considered in Parts 2 and 3, below. Details of the distribution of wall-types, and what they reveal about the process of enclosure and land management, feature in Part 4.

Part 2. Routeways

The course and use of Hebden's various routeways has been recorded and is described below, broadly in chronological sequence.[13] In today's landscape some routeways take the form of rights of way (macadamised roads, footpaths and bridle ways), others can be identified in the field as relic green lanes, droving funnels or holloways. Some represent through routes; others service - or have serviced - local requirements. Reviewing their course and role also demonstrates the importance of routeways as aids to understanding structural and functional relationships within an historical landscape.

2.1. Prehistoric to medieval

Hebden village is located where through routes running east/west and north/south intersect and where there are crossing points of beck and river (Beaumont *et al*, 2003). The modern B6265 Pateley Bridge to Grassington Road follows the course of a trans-Pennine route that is probably of prehistoric origin. Through the ages Hebden has afforded the first (or last) staging post for travellers crossing the inhospitable moorland over the watershed between Wharfedale and Nidderdale. Between Greenhow Hill and Grassington the modern road (B6265) follows the North Craven Fault, where limestone provides a natural 'causeway', flanked on the higher ground by poorly-drained peaty deposits overlying gritstones and rocks of the Yoredale Series (Edwards and Trotter 1954, 26, Fig 10).[14]

Early use of the east/west route is implied by the occurrence of prehistoric sites lying in Appletreewick township, parallel to the present road-line. Artefacts from the Mesolithic period have been found at Greenhow, close to Stump Cross (the name suggesting a boundary- or waymarker). There are also cup-marked rocks and the kerbstones of a small Bronze Age burial mound (Walker 1956; Feather 1964). The latter aligns with two similar monuments close to Scar Top House on the edge of Hebden Moor (Raistrick 1964). The route continues westwards, following a sight-line to a fold in the hills and dip in the horizon, where it passes close to the so-called Druids' altar at Bordley and heads towards the Roman marching camp on Mastiles Lane (White 2002, 25, 36, Figs 14, 22). Further evidence of the use of the east/west route during the Romano-British period derives from the find near Greenhow of a pig of smelted lead, dated from the reign of Emperor Trajan (AD 98-117), (Raistrick 1933; Wilson 2003, 49).

To the east of Hebden village, skeins of holloways can be seen lying between the SE and NE primary enclosures; they lie on either side of the modern road as it heads down Hebden Bank towards the beck. Their disposition suggests the beck was forded in the immediate vicinity of the village, long before there was a single bridging point. Westwards from the beck the 'old' through route apparently crossed Town Hill, traversing the northernmost part of the village. It continued along a well-marked holloway

and droving funnel through the field named Sykes, lying between the SW and NW primary enclosures. The route then divided, evidence of its branches surviving as footpaths and green tracks. One branch headed towards Grassington village. Another followed a more northerly course to Conistone, Upper Wharfedale, Littondale and Langstrothdale, or via Kilnsey and Mastiles Lane to Malham, west Craven, and beyond. A third branch remained within the bounds of the township, passing along Tinkers' Lane and a limb of Hebden Moor lying between the western boundary of the NW enclosure and the shared boundary of township and stinted pasture (Figs 22, 23, 25, 36, 39).

Our observations confirm the close association between the perimeter boundaries of primary enclosures and the routeways that lie outside them. They are consistent with Mary Atkin's description (1982/3; 1993, 148, 150) of roads and tracks circumventing primary enclosures including (in the Kendal area) a major drove road for Scottish cattle named Galloway-gate. Stout boundaries were required to prevent animals in transit from straying onto cultivated land and meadow and destroying valuable resources. It is highly likely that Hebden's primary enclosures similarly reflect its situation on a through route. The date of their formation is unknown, although the nature of their boundaries suggests that they could be medieval, but may be earlier (*cf* findings at Roystone Grange). The need for stock-proof barriers surely became acute *c*1200, when Simon de Hebden, lord of the manor, granted a charter to Fountains Abbey conferring the right to

'free transit through all his land of Hebbedene (except corn and meadow) for themselves, their men, and sheep in going and returning from shearing and for their other cattle when they wish, with carriage. And when they wish to unyoke ... or to feed their sheep and cattle, they may remain one night, or two if necessary' (Lancaster 1915, vol 1, 350).

Similar grants were made by other manorial lords in Upper Wharfedale, underlining the impact of this twice-annual transhumance. It involved the movement of thousands of animals, principally sheep, from their winter pastures near the Abbey and in Nidderdale to extensive summer grazing grounds around Malham and westwards into the Lake District. Moorhouse (2003, 336-41) instances flock sizes in excess of 15,000 in the thirteenth century. Fleeces clipped or collected on the grange at Kilnsey (the Fountains Abbey centre for west Craven) were carted in wagons to Fountains (Collinson 1994, 41; Raistrick 1980).

Other routes, also in use during the medieval period, passed southwards through Hebden village. Holloways running down Hebden Bank and Low Green presumably led to where the beck could be forded. This route then passed between the southernmost extent of the toft compartment and Hall Garth, joining Back Lane at the head of Lythe Flatt Lane ('Flat' on OS maps), (Figs 26, 27). One branch provided access to parts of the SW primary enclo-

---

[13] Observations by T. Hannam-Whitham and L. Walker (HHG).
[14] Observation by R.A. Stockdale (HHG).

sure; another to a crossing of the River Wharfe. Referred to in a Fountains Abbey charter of *c* 1240, (Lancaster 1915 vol 2, 729) 'the ford at Hebbedene' probably lay a short distance upstream from the confluence of Hebden Beck and the River Wharfe, close to the present site of the hippings (stepping stones) and a footbridge built in the late nineteenth century (Fig 44). Details in the thirteenth century charter link Hebden and neighbouring Thorpe; the ford also provided access to Burnsall and lower Wharfedale, as well as Skipton and Airedale.

Consistent with manorial custom, the township's moorland grazing grounds were served by a droveway which originated in the heart of the village: it ran upstream beside the beck along High Green (*ie* between the NE and NW enclosures), then by-passed Hole Bottom hamlet and continued up the steep ascent known as Hebden Raikes (from *hraca*, OE, rough, narrow path; cattle or sheep walk), (Smith 1961, 1962).[15] Wall patterns reveal a large wooded enclosure (Waite Scars) bordering the raikes to the east, and intakes from moorland (previously part of the stinted pasture) lying to the west. Intaking took place in two stages (*ie* during periods of pre- and post-parliamentary enclosure), resulting in the formation of two droving funnels running 'in series' north/south. Although no longer in use, the walling pattern survives and hence the funnels remain visible in the landscape (Figs 25, 36, 37, 45).

Before 1856, miners living in Hebden used the route up the raikes to reach the extensive lead-workings on Grassington Moor. The Hebden Moor Mining Company was responsible for engineering an alternative route, running up the eastern side of the beck above Hole Bottom hamlet. The beck was bridged (Fig 46) and the hillside beneath Hebden Scar was levelled to form a track leading to the company's mines and processing areas around Bolton Gill.

Another droveway, namely Hartlington Raikes, lay just outside Hebden's eastern township boundary and the SE primary enclosure (Fig 25). It served the eastern side of Hebden Moor and Hebden High Moor, where the manor of Hartlington shared grazing rights.

2.2. The Pateley Bridge to Grassington turnpike and after

The turnpike trust was created by Act of Parliament in 1758 and construction began two years later (Wright1985, 165). With the coming of the turnpike the swathe of land occupied by the earlier routeway was replaced by a much narrower drained and surfaced road bordered, to the east of the village, by an infill of newly-created enclosures [*eg* Home Field, High Side, Why Gap Meadow (Figs 28, 31, 42)]. The modern road exactly follows the line of the turnpike.

Prior to the advent of the turnpike the 'old' single-track Wapentake bridge carried the east/west route across the beck. The earliest known reference occurs in a Quarter Sessions record of 1631, making the case for a replacement. Emphasis is placed on the significance of its situation:

'The inhabitants of Hebden in Craven, as also many of the King's subjects in their travel, have sustained much delayment and have had great hindrance in their journeys by reason of the decay of a bridge in Hebden being lately driven down with the violence of a great flood, which bridge stood in the common Rode Way between most parts of Craven and the markett townes of Ripon, Knaresborough and the cittye of York' (cited by Joy *et al* 2002, 37).

Still in place and providing access to Brook Street, the present structure was built in 1757. About three years later an additional bridge was built some 50m downstream to carry the new turnpike road. Simultaneously the east/west route was re-aligned - an alignment that was retained after the turnpike ceased to operate (*c* 1822). Thus in 1827 the road level was raised and the decaying turnpike bridge was replaced by the present, impressive, county road bridge (Figs 47, 50).[16]

A further consequence of the establishment of the turnpike was to by-pass and supersede the older route across Town Hill and along the droving funnel between the SW and NW primary enclosures (see above). Thus on the western side of the bridge the turnpike road cut through part of the toft compartment, disrupting its layout. Continuing towards Grassington it ran through the SW primary enclosure, failing to respect its perimeter boundary (Figs 32, 33). A turnpike milestone survives on the roadside verge, some 100m west of the Hebden/Grassington township boundary, confirming that this section of the modern B6265 follows the course of the earlier road (Raistrick 1971, 117-18).

Other modifications to Hebden's road pattern date from the seventeenth to nineteenth centuries. Access to the river crossing and the corn and textile mills changed when Back Lane and Lythe Flatt Lane were downgraded in favour of Main Street and Mill Lane, respectively. The date of Mill Lane is uncertain (but see below). Main Street is surprisingly late: it does not appear on either the tithe map or OS 1st edition 6" map and hence must date from the second half of the nineteenth century. It was created from that part of the village green bordering the eastern margin of the toft compartment. The fact that Main Street was built on common land may account for its unusual width, bringing a sense of spaciousness to the village centre (Fig 56).

2.3. Compartments in the landscape

Mapping the course of routeways, and relating them to those field boundaries judged to be the oldest, has enabled us to define compartments both within and outside the nuclear village. Furthermore, consideration of the boundaries, internal features and functional significance of each compartment has drawn attention to features in the contemporary landscape that relate to the past, and particularly to Hebden as a manorial settlement. These observations are reviewed in Part 3. Additional evidence relating to the process of enclosure and land-use, during both the manorial and post-manorial periods, is presented in Part 4.

---

[15] Unless otherwise indicated, field and other local names are taken from the Hebden TAM and title deeds; interpretations are from Smith 1961 and 1962 (see bibliography). The two volumes are used in tandem: 1961 lists place- and field names; 1962 provides an interpretative list of name elements. Abbreviations: OE=Old English, ON=Old Norse, ME=Middle English, OFr= Old French).
[16] Plans and Documents on Hebden Bridges, Quarter Sessions Records QS1, 96/1 (1757) QD3/61 (1826); West Yorkshire County Record Office (WYCRO), Wakefield.

Figure 1. Hebden village looking north from the River Wharfe to Great Whernside. The nuclear village is aligned to the beck and surrounded by a zone of irregular enclosures with a scattering of farms and outbarns up to the moorland fringe. The Hebden/ Grassington boundary passes through the grounds of Grassington Hospital (left margin), now demolished; from the centre of the print the boundary runs eastwards under the cloud shadow. © *Copyright reserved Cambridge University Collection of Air Photographs, AWJ 27.*

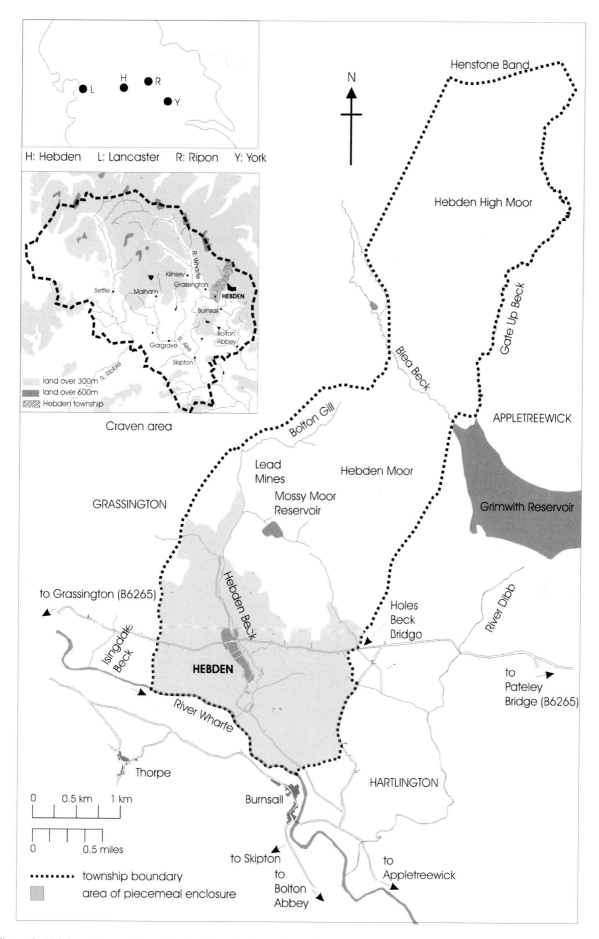

Figure 2. Hebden village and township: location, territory and terrain.
The River Wharfe, Hebden Beck, the B6265 and Mossy Moor reservoir (built between1850 and1857) are included to assist orientation.

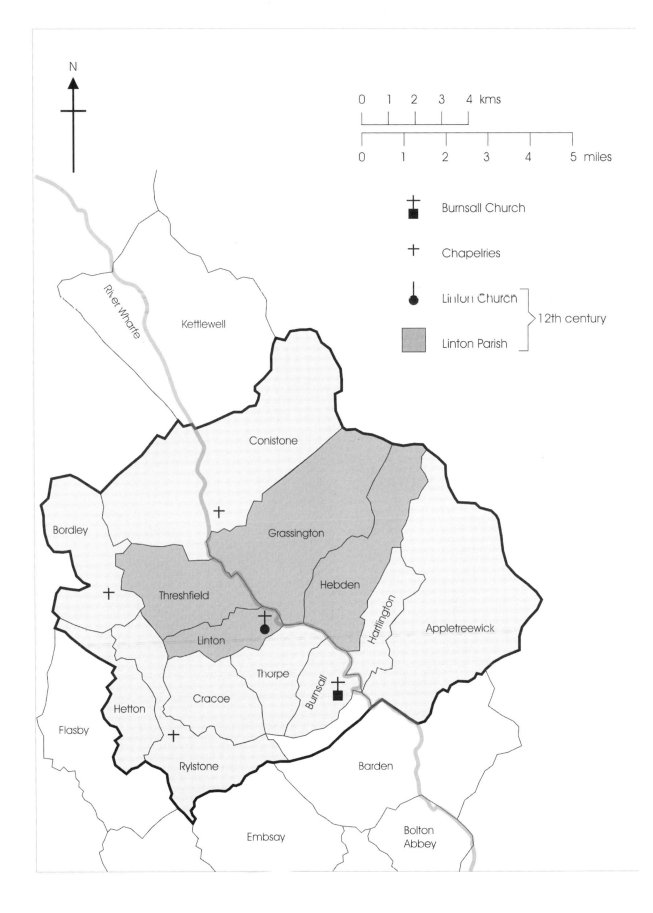

Figure 3. Townships in Upper Wharfedale thought to have formed the Anglo-Saxon estate and parish of Burnsall, with chapelries at Rylstone, Bordley and Conistone; the constituents of Linton Parish are also shown.

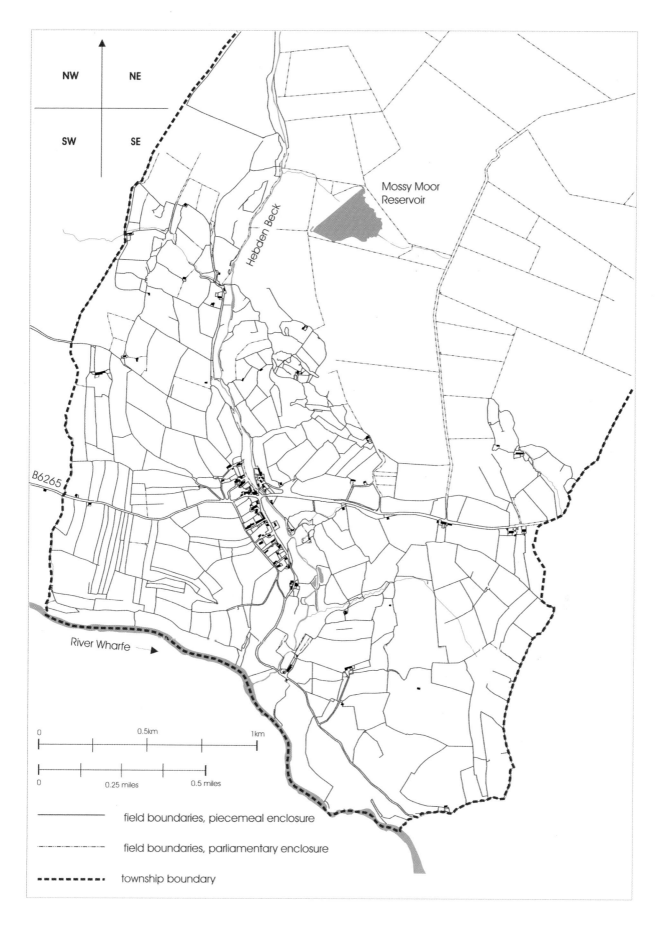

Figure 4. Field boundaries as shown on the tithe map (1847) and first edition 6" OS map (1857); also the southernmost allotments created by Act of Parliament (1857) as shown on the Enclosure map and the 6" OS map, second edition (1910). The course of Hebden Beck and the B6265 were used to divide our recording area into four quadrants: *ie* south-east (SE), south-west (SW), north-west (NW) and north-east (NE).

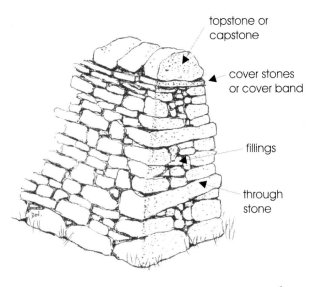
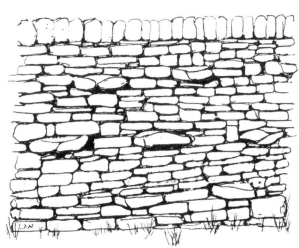

topstone or
capstone

cover stones
or cover band

fillings

through
stone

a, b

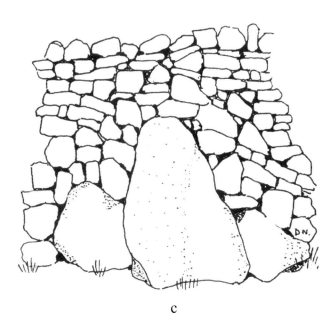

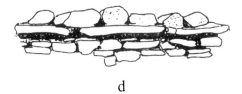

d

c

Figure 5. Hebden's walls: **a,b**, as constructed under the enclosure act (Group 5), without and with projecting through stones; **c,d**, features of walls classified as Group 1, *eg* incorporation of natural boulders; unilaterally-projecting through stones under random topstones (detail). Drawings by Dorothy Newall, HHG.

Figure 6. Hebden's walls: **a**, wall marking the township boundary and stinted pasture (bordering Hebden Moor and Tinkers' Lane; see Figure 39); b, irregular wall (Group 3); **c**, regular wall. Drawings by Dorothy Newall, HHG.

Figure 7. Wall built under the Enclosure Act (1857) and bounding Backstone Edge Lane (see Fig 42); illustrating differences in the character of stone cf. Fig 8, denoting local variations in geology. See also Fig 8.

Figure 8. See legend for Fig 7

Figure 9. Walling quarry seen from Backstone Edge Lane.

Figure 10. Crawthorns, SW primary enclosure, showing the close association between tumbled walling, aged hawthorns and mature ash trees (boundaries classified as Group 1). The fence divides a strip field previously in dual ownership.

Figure 11. Crawthorns: limestone wall with orthostats; the lintel of a filled-in sheep-creep can be seen to the right.

Figure 12. Boundary wall of NW primary enclosure beside the droveway along High Green, with orthostatic and recumbent boulders and a course of protruding through stones beneath the topstones (Group 1).

Figure 13. Another section of the wall shown in Figure 12, illustrating its sinuous course along an embankment.

Figure 14. Hebden Scar, NE quadrant; wall incorporating random boulders.

Figure 15. External boundary wall (Group 2) at a wall head. (Cane height 1.3m, 4ft).

Figure 16. External boundary wall at a wall head with township boundary marker; also weathered inscription (initials or mason mark?) just above the wall base.

Figure 17. Irregular wall (Group 3) forming a property boundary inside the NW primary enclosure, illustrating its wavering course and natural or roughly-shaped topstones that protrude bilaterally *c*. 50mm (2 in) beyond the wall-face.

Figure 18. Wall on Scarside (NE quadrant), showing orthostats and boulders stabilising a stepped wall base and possibly placed to fill gaps in a hawthorn hedge.

Figure 19. NW primary enclosure; irregular wall (Group 3), largely composed of weathered stone obtained from field clearance (Cane height 1.3m, 4ft). See also Fig 20.

Figure 20. NW primary enclosure: irregular wall (Group 3); see legend to Fig 19.

Figure 21. Regular wall (Group 4) forming a field subdivision and created between 1853 and 1910 on map evidence.

Figure 22. Wide holloway and droving funnel in 'Sykes', looking east towards Town Head farm (see Figures 35 and 39) and lying between the walled boundary of the NW primary enclosure (left) and the remains of a hedged boundary on the perimeter of the SW primary enclosure (right).

Figure 23. Blocked exit from Sykes: the cross-wall shows a characteristic 'dip' where it has been built across the holloway. The main droving route passed between Garnshaw farm (left) and Pickering End farmhouse (right).

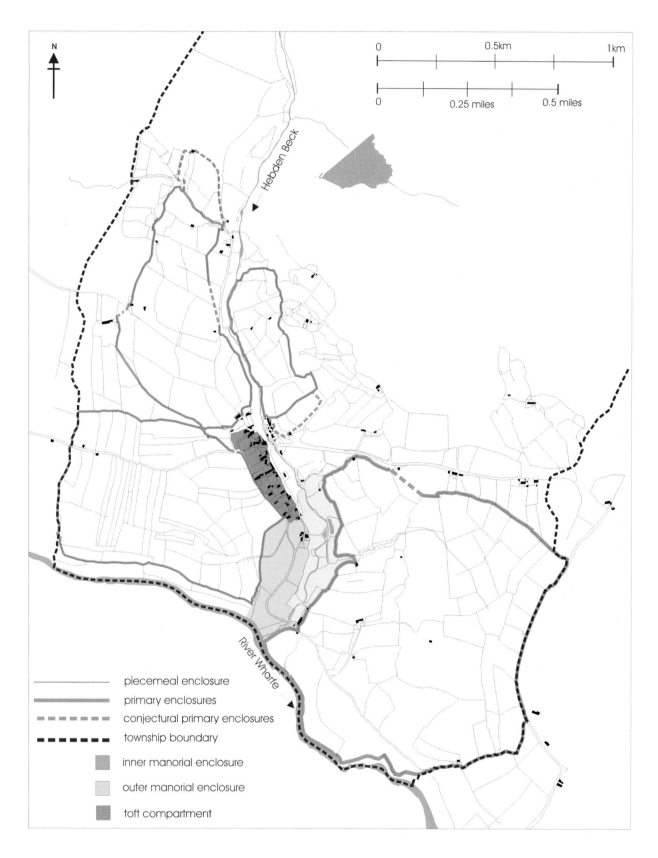

Figure 24. Early results of the survey of field boundaries, revealing four primary enclosures within the pre-Enclosure landscape and compartments within the nuclear village.

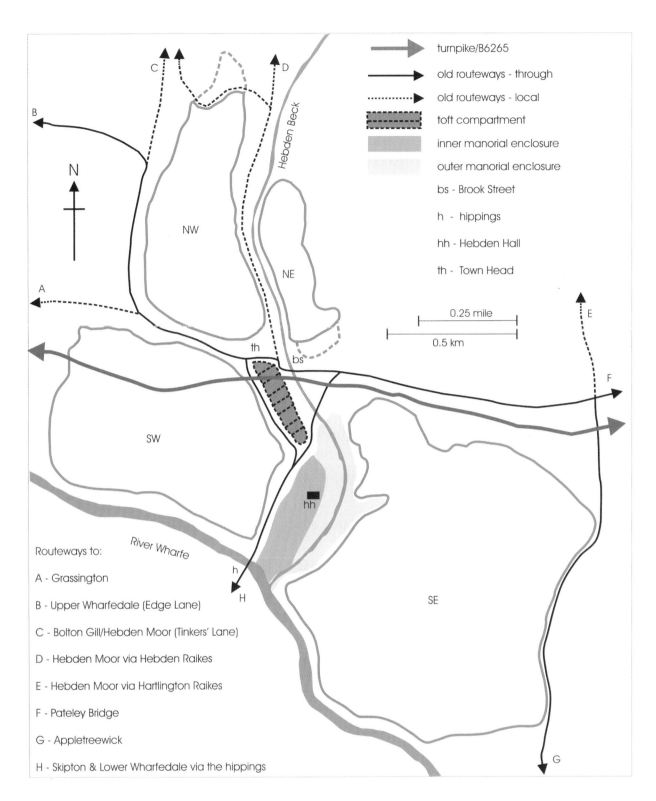

Figure 25. Diagrammatic representation of the lay-out and destination of routeways and their relationship to the perimeter boundaries of the four primary enclosures and compartments within the village. Also provides a model on which to base a consideration of the layout of Hebden during the manorial period.

Figure 26. The nuclear village. For interpretation, see Figure 27.
Aerial photograph reproduced by kind permission of Ordnance Survey. © Crown Copyright. NC/04/24872.

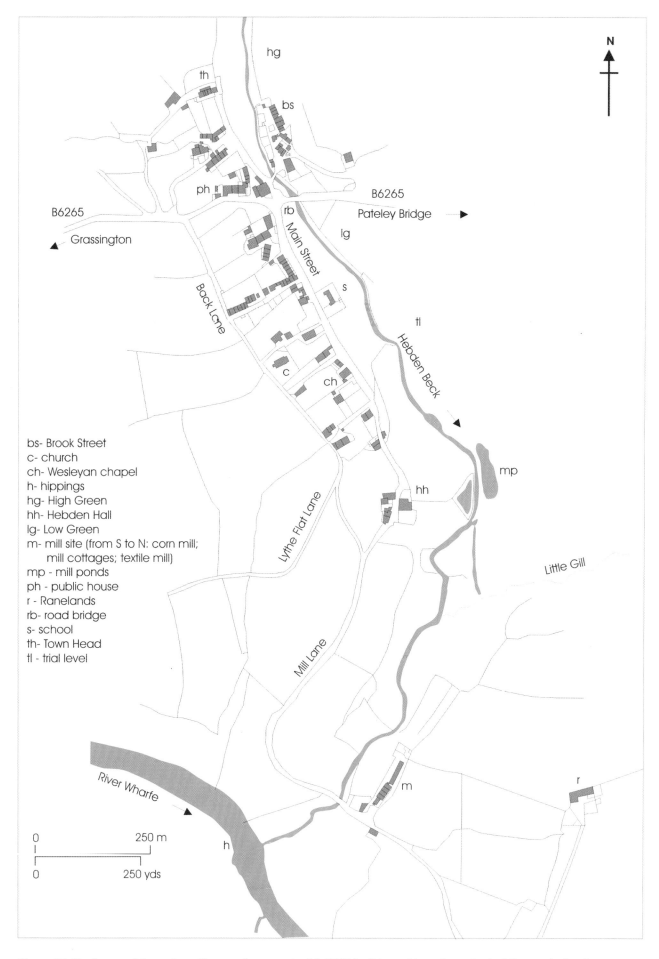

Figure 27. The layout of the nuclear village as shown on the OS 6"1910 edition, with roads, tracks, buildings and other features mentioned in the text.

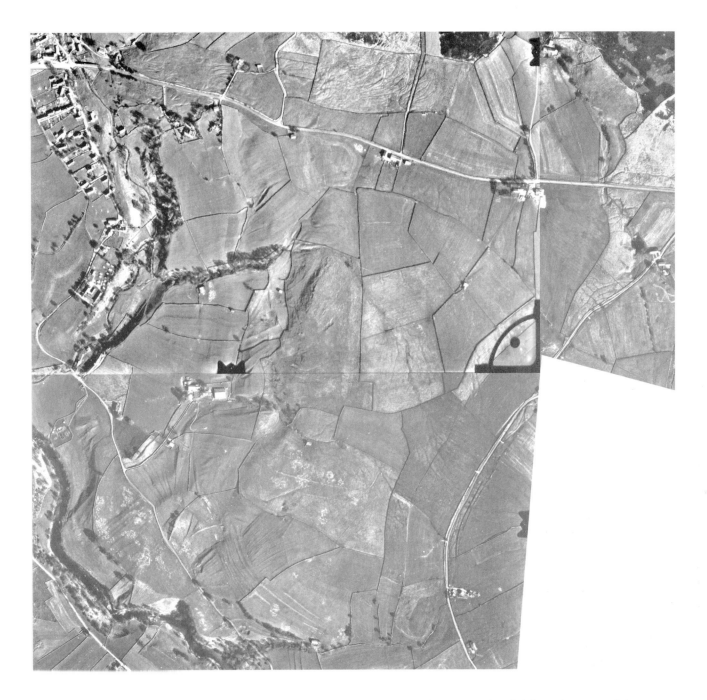

Figure 28. The SE primary enclosure and the line of the modern road to the east of the village, where it follows the course of the turnpike. *Aerial photograph reproduced by kind permission of Ordnance Survey. © Crown Copyright. NC/04/24872.*

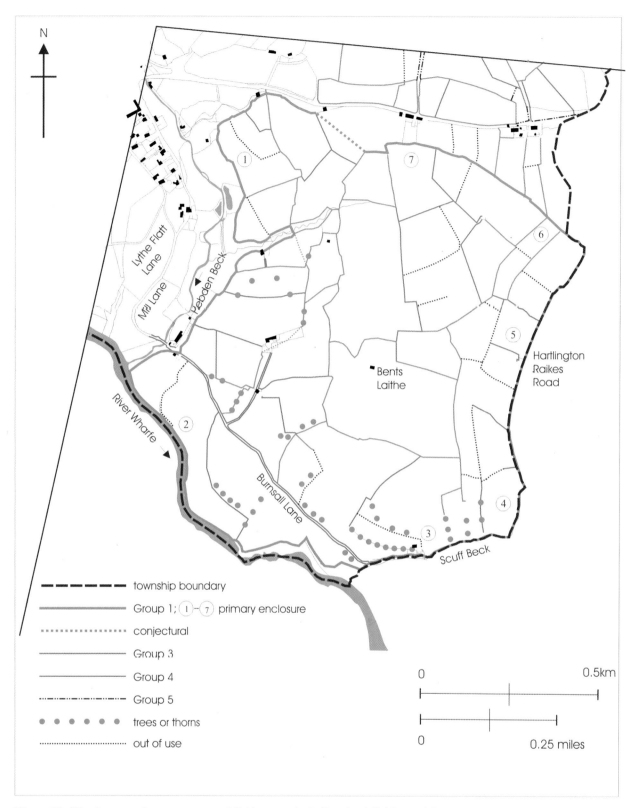

Figure 29. SE primary enclosure: outcome of field survey, including the definition and features of the perimeter boundary (see Appendix 1 for details) and classification of field boundaries.

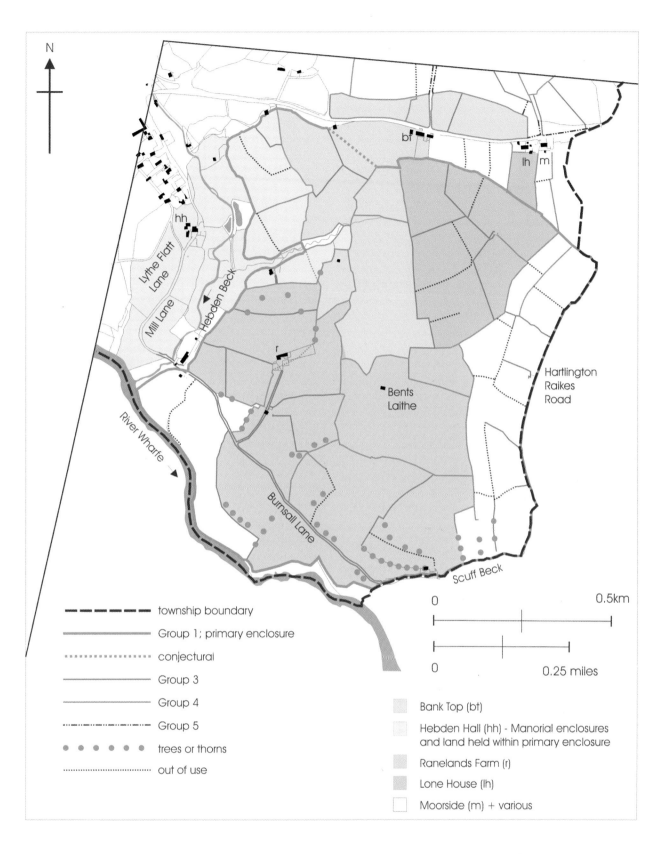

Figure 30. SE primary enclosure; classification of field boundaries and ownership of land (TAM).

Part 3: Manorial Hebden: a model

Clearly, the scarcity of documentary evidence - particularly that relating to manorial Hebden - precludes absolute dating and the formulation of a secure chronological account of settlement and agricultural organisation. However, the definition of compartments within the landscape has enabled us to formulate a working hypothesis in the form of a model. The use of models to explore early landscape development is advocated by Williamson (2003b, 198), who considers that 'models and guesswork are indispensable when direct evidence is in short supply'. The use of data pertaining to past and present conditions to model the past (the retrogressive approach) is similarly commended by Roberts and Wrathmell (2002, 4). These authors (1998, 99) also point out the shortcomings of synoptic maps or models, which compress time into a single plane and hence tend to over-simplify and obscure developmental sequences. Despite this caveat, we are satisfied that our study provides useful pointers to past patterns of organisation in the Hebden landscape (Figs 24-27) as well as a basis for defining phased sequences of development (*eg* the process of enclosure) which can be putatively dated.

The existence of a scattering of individual farms and small hamlets around the periphery of the SE, NW and NE primary enclosures (Fig 43) is backed by evidence from deeds of title of the seventeenth and eighteenth centuries. This suggests that settlement may originally have been dispersed, with the later superimposition of a nuclear village - a pattern found elsewhere in Craven (Roberts and Wrathmell 2002, 109). We have shown that the east/west through-route that preceded the turnpike effectively divided northern and southern sectors of both the agricultural and built landscapes, helping to define distinct compartments. Core elements within the southern sector comprise Hebden Hall, the manorial enclosures and mill; also a planned toft compartment elements that relate to the SE and SW primary enclosures, respectively. In addition, a smaller component of the village (north of the 'old' east/west route) is thought to have formed a small, irregular but distinct unit that we name 'Town Head hamlet', with associated landholdings in the NW and NE primary enclosures.

3.1. Hall

The site of Hebden Hall is now occupied by a house divided into two dwellings, known as Hebden Hall and Manor House. The foundations of a medieval building remain under the lawn to the south of the present building, appearing in hot dry weather as scorch marks overlying limestone rubble. Traces of the small manorial fish-pond, mentioned by a local writer (Bland, *c* 1875, 21), can be seen in the croft to the south of the garden, where a low embankment surrounds a small depression in which a pool forms after rain.[17]

Our analysis of boundaries and routeways indicates that the Hall was situated inside its own double enclosure, lying between the SW and SE primary enclosures. The boundary of the inner manorial enclosure includes a grassed bank and embanked hedgerows encompassing Hall Garth and the croft where the fish-pond is located. The outer manorial enclosure extends across Hebden Gill where its boundary, coterminous with that of the SE primary enclosure, additionally contains the site of the manorial corn mill (TAM). The SE primary enclosure, which probably included demesne land, was contiguous with the manorial enclosures; field divisions and markings suggest it was managed as part pasture, part arable and/or meadow. The boundaries of inner and outer manorial enclosures are also coterminous to the south-west, along the border of Lythe Flat Lane, respecting the boundaries of the manorial enclosures and where a species-rich hedgerow suggests a long-established boundary. In contrast, Mill Lane cuts across the manorial enclosures and has a length of hedgerow with fewer species, implying that this route was established at a later date. Inspection of the arch of the mill bridge which crosses the beck shows that it is in two parts: originally a packhorse bridge, it was subsequently widened to take wheeled traffic.[18]

3.2. Toft compartment

Our observations are consistent with Roberts' view that the layout of Hebden conforms to that of a single row toft compartment created during the manorial period (Sheppard 1966; Roberts 1987,1990; *cf* Moorhouse 2003, 306), (Figs 26, 27). It comprised a sequence of eight relatively small enclosures, each with a house-plot, outbuildings and green area, and lay between Back Lane to the west and the village green to the east. That part of the green adjacent to the toft compartment is named Kiln Green (First ed. 6" OS map); the grassed-over remains of the communal corn-drying kiln can be identified, lying to the north of the nineteenth century school building. Following well-established precedents elsewhere, we assume that the toft compartment originally accommodated servile peasants who were succeeded by tenant farmers, then (in the particular circumstances pertaining to Hebden), freeholders.

Beyond Back Lane, in the SW primary enclosure, there are wall lines which are bowed, form aratral curves, or bound long, narrow fields, reflecting patterns of medieval cultivation and indicating that, prior to enclosure it was a common arable field. Back Lane, a frequently-occurring feature of toft compartments, provided access to part of the arable field as well as a through route running north/south to a forded crossing of the Wharfe. Thus the components of Hebden manor, and their disposition, accord with the 'hall-and-hamlet' arrangement described by Mary Atkin (1993), with the hall or a large farm holding a large pasture oval and farms in the toft compartment having land within a smaller, arable enclosure.

---

[17] Observation by J. Stockdale (HHG); confirmed by S. Moorhouse whose advice is gratefully acknowledged.
[18] Observation by T. Hannam-Whitham (HHG).

3.3. Town Head hamlet

Contrary to Robert's inference that Hebden's toft compartment occupied the whole of the nuclear village (1987, 36-7), we consider that Town Head hamlet comprised a small but distinct settlement. It consisted of Town Head farm with houses and a green on Town Hill situated west of the beck, with present-day Brook Street to the east. In the mid-nineteenth century inhabitants of Town Head hamlet held land in the NW and NE primary enclosures (TAM). These observations again accord with those of Mary Atkin: she confirms that where there is more than one pair of primary enclosures, there are instances where a second settlement unit exists, adjacent to the first but separate from it, the two also being distinguishable by forms of tenure.[19] Earthworks in the fields immediately north of Town Head farm suggest a settlement site that predates the planned manorial village (see Part 4).

Thus our field observations, supported by evidence from elsewhere in the north of England, are consistent with the thesis that the southern sector of Hebden's contemporary landscape echoes a planned landscape of the medieval period (but possibly or probably overlying earlier settlement forms). The aetiology of elements in the northern sector is less certain. In both instances, however, understanding is assisted by an examination of patterns of organisation and management in the agricultural and built environments during the medieval and post-medieval periods and throughout the township (see Part 4).

[19] M. Atkin (*pers comm*): Croston township (Lancs.) evidently contained two distinct settlement units, Croston village and Drinkhouse(s), each with its own common arable field and meadow.

Part 4: Management strategies and evolution of the agricultural landscape

A retrospective view of the distribution of landholdings and the management of assets and resources during the manorial period has been gleaned from various documentary sources. There are records relating to the transfer of the manor to freeholders, plus others from the late sixteenth and early seventeenth centuries that convey information about land use and management. In addition, deeds of title from the seventeenth and eighteenth centuries offer clues to the sequence of enclosure and development of the agricultural landscape. Described by Wrathmell (2003, 33) as 'a type of record whose value for agrarian history has been consistently underestimated', the latter also refer to common rights (Winchester 2000). Taken together, these sources illuminate management strategies vested in freeholders. At the same time, they demonstrate the longevity of manorial custom - while also legislating for its continuance.

4.1. Landholdings

In 1589, when lordship of the manor passed from the Tempest family (via their mortgagees) to three freeholders (William Toppan, Peter Blande and Robert Eshe) the manor comprised 30 messuages, two cottages and a water mill, 'with lands there'.[20] 'Lands' generally refers to strips in a common arable field. Less than a decade later (in 1598) a one-third holding of the manor was relinquished and divided equally between the two remaining trustee freeholders (Joy *et al* 2002, 31).[21] The agreement specifies 'the particular pcells of lande houses and meadowes of that halfe pte or moyitie of one messuage in Hebden.' Of the twenty-seven named 'pcells' (or 'parcells'), the largest comprise one acre or half an acre, but most are only a rod or rood (quarter of an acre), or half a rood. Some field names correspond to those found on the nineteenth century TAM, situated in various locations around the village (*eg* Flatts, Cross thornes, Sourelande, Bentte); they are also specified as lying within the West or East Fields or Sedbar or Sedber (*ie* within the SW, SE and NW primary enclosures). Open field agriculture continued in Hebden for at least a century and a half after acquisition of the manor by freeholders: for instance, there is reference in a deed of 1754 to a farmholding with 'several pieces and parcels of land lying dispersedly in the common fields of Hebden'.[22] The spreading of an individual's holdings within the open fields was designed to achieve an equitable distribution of good and poor land.

There are various manifestations of change within the manorial holding after ownership passed to freeholders. A deed of 1689/90 refers to Hebden Hall as the 'new dwelling house', providing an approximate date for its rebuilding in stone.[23] Another deed (1721/2) concerns 'All that East End or Part of all the Capitall Messuage or Dwelling house ... called Hebden Hall'; it usefully provides details of the landholding.[24] It also links ownership of 'one moiety or half part of Hebden Hall' with 'one halfe part of... all that formerly stinted pasture called Hebden pasture'. We infer that 'formerly' refers to a stinted pasture that occupied much of the SE enclosure and antedated the moorland pasture enclosed *c* 1600. Thus a proportion of the old pasture was held as demesne, with the remainder granted to occupants of the toft compartment. A reference to grazing rights on 'the old inclosed pasture ... held of the Chief Lord of the fee by suit and service' appears in a deed of 1636 recording a transfer of land held by Green House, a farm within the toft compartment.[25] Mention elsewhere of 'the corn pasture' (1670) implies that animals were grazed on arable land after harvest; other details suggest it lay in the East Field).[26]

4.2. Legacy of common rights

References to common rights held by Hebden freeholders suggest a continuation of systems that classically originated with, and were administered by, the manor court. As well as controlling the allocation and use of land within the common fields, manor courts were also responsible for regulating grazing and access to the resources necessary for everyday living. The latter generally included wood (for building, implements and fuel), peat (for fuel), bracken (bedding for stock), stone and turves (for building) and ling for thatch (Winchester 2000, 32-33, 45-46, 66-68, 78-79. 123-42).

In Hebden, as elsewhere, intercommoning took place on the outer fringes of the township before territorial stock-proof boundaries became established. Grazing was shared with Grassington to the west and Hartlington to the east. Instigated *c* 1600 by the new freeholders, the enclosure of intermediate moorland (*ie* at an altitude of 300 to 360m) and its designation as stinted pasture was a significant development. It is referred to as 'the now enclosed pasture of Hebden' in two documents of the period that relate to a dispute between Hebden and Hartlington over rights of pasture and turbary. Coterminosity of the boundaries of the stinted pasture and sections of the Hebden/ Hartlington and Hebden/ Grassington township boundaries have been discussed elsewhere (Beaumont *et al* 2004, 70-71, 74-77). A further indication of the extent of the stinted

---

[20] see **fn 6**.

[21] From a deed of 1598, previously in the collection of Arthur Raistrick and transcribed by D Joy *c*.1966; see D Joy *et al* 2002. (The whereabouts of the original is no longer known.)

[22] West Yorkshire County Record Office, Registry of Deeds (WYCRO - RD), Wakefield: AI 546/703 (1754).

[23] North Yorkshire County Record Office (NYCRO), Northallerton: ZXF 1/10 (1689/90).

[24] WYCRO - RD: R52/79 (1721/2).

[25] NYCRO: ZXF 1/10, Mic. 2626 (1636).

[26] Raistrick MS 603 (1670), Skipton Reference Library.

pasture is provided by references to 'Blaibeck' (marking its northern limit; Fig 2) and a later reference (1724) to the siting of peat pits in locations recognised today.[27]

Other references to pasture rights concern the control of grazing both within and outside this stinted pasture. They further specify that only animals held within the manor were commonable and permit 'the going driving keeping and feeding of all manner of Beasts Horses Sheep and Cattle Levant & Couchant'.[28] This formula, found almost exclusively in manor court documents in the Lake District and North Pennines, limited the number of stock grazed to the number that could be sustained through the winter on the produce of each holding (Winchester 2000, 79-82). In addition, title deeds for property in Hebden consistently show that grazing rights were allocated in proportion to an 'ancient yearly rent' paid by each landholder. For example, a deed of 1777 relating to Green House ('one messuage or dwelling house') and its attached grazings, is specifically linked to the payment of an ancient yearly rent (in this instance 5s. 8d). The latter applies 'throughout all that Great Inclosure and Stinted Pasture ... commonly called Hebden Pasture' and also 'upon and throughout all that Outcommon, Moors, Mosses, Wastes and Waste Grounds of Hebden, not now inclosed' (ie before parliamentary enclosure). The annual payment additionally gave access to those natural resources and necessities available from the common (stinted) pasture and unenclosed out-commons.[29]

As well as providing another example of the perpetuation of manorial custom, payment of the ancient yearly rent established a system of proportionality that applied to landholdings throughout the township. Significantly it also qualified freeholders to a *pro rata* share of the 'Royalties, rights, profits [and] perquisites' of the manor.[30] Continued into the nineteenth century, this included the right to royalties from the lead industry, with payments to each freeholder also being calculated in proportion to their ancient yearly rent.

Timber or estovers was a further resource to which common rights usually applied. They appear to be absent from Hebden deeds, suggesting that woodland had been severely depleted by the late seventeenth or early eighteenth centuries. (In contrast, freeholders still enjoy rights of turbary.) Contemporary woodland is sparse and generally unprotected from the ravages of sheep, cattle, and rabbits. As illustrated on aerial photographs, it is largely restricted to the steep sides of Hebden Beck and its tributaries (Figs 1, 28, 36). However, the little that remains, plus some woodland names, provide clues to its earlier distribution.

Relic woodland in Hebden Gill extends northwards for about 2km beyond High Green; it principally comprises hazel, ash, rowan, alder, and a few oaks and hollies. Strips

of woodland are also associated with Paradise Beck, Little Gill and Skuff Beck (from *skogr*, ON, or *scogh*, ME, wood); (see also Gelling and Cole 2003, 248). Although woodland was generally protected by enclosure (eg Waite Scars, recently replanted; Fig 39), many walls have now collapsed. Coppice stools occur infrequently and such old pollards as remain are rapidly depleting. Thus it appears that the active management of woodland ceased long ago. On the south-western edge of the township the name Garnshaw, or its alternative Garnshay, (both derived from *sceaga,* OE, copse or small wood) applies to a dispersed hamlet on the Hebden/Grassington boundary, where there was probably intercommoning; Higham (1988/9) describes a clutch of features associated with *shay* names, as found in the old West Riding (see below).

The name 'Standard' (ME, tree stump) occurs in relation to moorland both north and south of Blea Beck. A palynological study confirms heavy tree cover on Hebden High Moor from *c* 4,790 BC (Mesolithic period) which was maintained to *c* 2,880 BC (late Neolithic) when there was an abrupt decline in trees and an influx of heather; the remains - mostly of birch- wood - are to be found in the lowermost levels of peat deposits. A gradual reduction in tree cover and an increase in shrubs and herbs continued through the Bronze and Iron Ages and into the nineteenth century (Atherden *et al*, in prep).

4.3. Lords, freeholders and enclosure

Information on ownership and landholdings has largely been derived from deeds of title, supplemented by data from land tax assessments (seventeenth to early nineteenth centuries), the TAM and EAM, and from census returns (1841-1901).[31,32] Field patterns and the sequence of walling, plus field names drawn from the TAM, assist in tracing earlier land-use and provide clues to the manner in which agriculture was organised. (For a comprehensive over-view of farming in the sixteenth century, see Overton 1996, especially pages 21-46).

4.3.1. Hall and SE primary enclosure
(Figs 28-31)

From our survey of field boundary types and wall abutments we conclude that partitioning of the SE primary enclosure took place in stages and over a long period of time, with the earliest field boundaries provisionally categorised as medieval and the process only reaching completion in the early nineteenth century. An early internal boundary, largely composed of robust boulder walling incorporating orthostats and associated with a few trees (Group 1) lies between 'Rainge Lands' and Ratlock Hill (Kecklocks on the TAM,[33]). It may represent the first head dyke: *ie* the

[27] WYCRO - RD: U 598/775 (1724).
[28] WYCRO - RD: CB 265/419 (1777).
[29] WYCRO - RD: BZ 723/961 (1777).
[30] WYCRO - RD: CB 265/419 (1777).
[31] WYCRO: Land Tax Assessments for Hebden.
[32] Census returns for Hebden, Skipton Reference Library: transcribed and interpreted by E. A. Bostock, M. Hargraves, P. Hodge, M. Holmes and J. Joy (HHG).
[33] M. Atkin (*pers comm*) cites G.Grigson 1987 *The Englishman's Flora*. Frome, 209, suggesting that *Kecklocks* is a local term for cow parsley. Note also O.Rackham (see bibliography: *Trees and Woodland,* 192, *Kex*): also, *eg, Kedlock* (Derbyshire), *Kelk* (Yorkshire, Durham and Northumberland).

outer boundary of the first stage in the formation of an oval enclosure, separating what was originally arable and/or meadow held in demesne from the (then unenclosed) common pasture (Roberts and Wrathmell 2002, 163). An alignment of Group 3 walls suggests a secondary expansion of the cultivated area, up the hillside. It is assumed that further extension of the perimeter boundary to the eastern township boundary represented the enclosure of a common pasture and the final stage in the formation of the SE primary enclosure, in the form recorded in this study.

Land within the SE primary enclosure, contiguous with the outer manorial enclosure and sharing a boundary running along the lip of Hebden Gill, is divided into closes, as is land bordering a small tributary valley called Little Gill. These are defined by a mix of boulder walls and walls of irregular construction. A deed of 1606 refers to 'all that selion of land or parsell of grounde called Little Gill in the field of Hebden'.[34] Little Gill also appears in a reference to Hebden Hall and it's holding (1721/2) and there are closes that still retain the name. The Hall also held Studfold (Studfield, TAM), a name linked with the breeding and keeping of horses, and a close traditionally known as Bull Coppy, ('Copy' on the TAM; from OFr, copeiz, coppice). This is where the community bull was housed, conveniently adjacent to the common pasture and his potential wives! Field names suggest that these enclosures were created during the manorial period and were attached to what became known as Manor Farm.

In addition, the area between Little Gill and the site of Ranelands farm may have been held in demesne as arable and/or meadow, subsequently becoming attached to Ranelands (TAM). A deed of 1714, concerns 'lands and grounds commonly called Rainge Lands ... lying or being in the East Field of Hebden (6 acres)'.[35] The name derives from ran (OE) or rein (ON), suggesting a boundary strip in an open arable field or, alternatively, land lying just outside a common pasture (Gambles 1995, 71): both are applicable. East Field is named in the deed of 1598. Gelling and Cole (2003, 269-71) deduce that where feld features in place-names, it often signifies open land, previously used for pasture but developing - during the latter part of the tenth century - to mean communally-cultivated arable. In Hebden, later use of the name East Field generally refers to that part of the primary enclosure lying south-east of Ranelands farm, known as Haws (TAM), (derivation OE, a hedge or encompassing fence, or a piece of ground enclosed or fenced in (Hooke 1998, 123).[36] It seems reasonable to suppose that in Hebden, as elsewhere, extension of the area of arable and/or meadow took place at a time of population expansion, although whether this was pre- or post-Conquest (ie late tenth, or late thirteenth to early fourteenth century) is uncertain. Overlying limestone and post-glacial deposits of sands and gravel, and having a favourable southerly aspect, Haws is characterised by evidence of lynchets and ridge and furrow, associated with several hedged boundaries. In an adjacent part of the East Field named Byland Dale, 'a parcel of land ... called Gales Lands' is referred to as 'lying in the common fields' (land, OE, tract of land, or strip of land in the common field.[37] Gales is a refence to the moisture-loving shrub Bog Myrtle or Sweet Gale (Gelling and Cole 2003; Gelling pers com).

The pattern of distribution of trees and thorns in field boundaries in Haws suggests that the best land was enclosed first, probably early in the post-manorial period, as the consolidation of strips got under way. Similar patterns are seen within the other primary enclosures. Deeds of the mid-eighteenth century also contain references to closes in the East Field, but these had disappeared by the time of the TAM, presumably as landholdings were reorganised. They were situated on either side of Burnsall Lane and include fields named Butts Brow (from ME, butte, an abutting strip of land), often denoting irregularly-shaped endpieces in a common field.

Ranelands is the only farm with its house and buildings situated inside the SE primary enclosure (Figs 30, 48). The earliest building was probably late seventeenth century and the landholding was enlarged by serial purchase (YVBSG 1999). The amalgamation of strips, completed in 1808, produced a holding of c 120ha (300a) that could be ring-fenced, subdivided and enclosed (TAM). The sequence in which walls were built can be deduced from their classification (irregular and regular) and abutments. The quantity of land attached to Ranelands increased further under the terms of the Enclosure Award with the addition of the outermost allotment on Hebden High Moor, extending to the Wharfedale/Nidderdale watershed and comprising some 240ha (600a).

Deeds from the eighteenth century refer to farms on the northern periphery of the SE enclosure, lying beside the east/west route (ie Bank Top, Lone House, Hebden Moorside). Most of their attached lands lay inside the SE primary enclosure, in sectors devoted to both arable and pasture. For example, Lone House held 'Two little pieces or parcells of land lying in the Hawes in the East Field of Hebden, one and a half rood' (1723).[38] A close called Brow (1.2ha; 3a) 'with one Laithe or Barn standing therein' is also named; it corresponds by name and description to closes and a laithe featured on the TAM and still identifiable. Walls inside the SE primary enclosure which partition the pasture-land held by Lone House are generally classified as regular (Group 4). An almost treeless landscape and the straight course of the walls suggests that they constitute a relatively late first generation of field boundaries. Land attached to each of the roadside farms is organised in blocks (TAM) and field names such as Cow Pasture and Bents recur, implying the earlier existence of common pasture and the relatively poor quality of some of the land. A number of field boundaries have gone out of use during the one hundred and fifty years that have elapsed between the tithe award and our field survey.

---

[34] Raistrick MS 600 (1606), Skipton Reference Library.
[35] WYCRO - RD: G 500/615 (1714).
[36] This interpretation relates to the South Midlands.
[37] WYCRO - RD: CC 609/811 (1731).
[38] WYCRO - RD: T 212/286 (1723).

4.3.2. Toft compartment and SW primary enclosure
(Figs 24-27, 32-35)

By analogy with other planned villages, we conclude that the toft compartment was created during the manorial period and, during the post-manorial period, was occupied by freeholders, described in deeds of the eighteenth century as yeomen.[39] Houses are south-facing and house plots originally bordered Kiln Green (ie until the creation of Main Street in the second part of the nineteenth century). Farm buildings and grassed garths, gardens and orchards lay towards Back Lane (YVBSG 1999, 5). Houses in the toft compartment retain architectural features characteristic of the vernacular style of the late seventeenth - early eighteenth centuries (eg inglenook fireplaces with integral bread-ovens); Green House carries a datestone (1674), (YVBSG 1999, 8-9). The regularity and character of the toft compartment has been partially disrupted, first by the creation of the turnpike, and second, by infill building in the nineteenth century and recently.

Now under grass, the SW primary enclosure shows clear indications of earlier field systems, providing ample evidence that it was a common arable field. Field-name elements such as land (see above) and flatt (OE and ON, division of the common field) appear on the TAM. Although it is cut by the turnpike/B6265, the arrangement of fields (recorded on the TAM and reflected in the contemporary pattern of field boundaries) suggests that the area within this primary enclosure is divided into four sectors, reflecting the history of ownership.

West Field (named in the deed of 1598) relates topographically to Back Lane and the toft compartment. Field markings and wall lines run predominantly east/west, aligned with the tofts; most echo the aratral curves or bowed lines of medieval ploughing (Fig 49). Moreover, the lack of an exact match between contemporary toft and field boundaries, on either side of Back Lane and apparent on the 1:25,000 OS map, probably denotes the earlier existence of selions (Roberts 1990, 114).

During the late seventeenth and eighteenth centuries references to closes began to replace 'pieces' or 'parcels' of ground in the West Field.[40] Thus, for example, enclosures named Lythe Flat and Lythe Flat Brow are specified in a document of 1693. And in 1761 one of the Lythe Flatts Closes (TAM) lying on a terrace above the River where the soil is of particularly good quality, is listed amongst 'several inclosed closes' (Lythe is from hlith, OE, ON, slope or hill-side).[41]

Most walled boundaries in the West Field, shown on the tithe map and surviving today, are classified as irregular (Group 3) and define ownership boundaries. Eighteenth century deeds and the TAM further show that almost all of the West Field, including Lythe Flatts, was held by farms in the toft compartment, the sequence of ownership of the enclosures or crofts largely corresponding to that of the tofts. This may point to the earlier existence of a Solskifte

(Rowley 1994, 35-6). The absence of trees from field boundaries suggests an extended period of open-field cultivation, with strip holdings being consolidated and internal, walled boundaries being established during the eighteenth century.

In contrast, the area known as Cross thornes (now Crawthorns), suggesting a secure fence, occupies a site where the land rises steeply to a knoll and limestone outcrops or lies close to the surface, limiting cultivation. Boundaries are characterised by the presence of hawthorns and ash trees growing along lines of boulders and tumbled walling that bound small closes (Figures 10, 11). Named in the deed of 1598, Crawthorns was subsequently multi-tenanted (references in deeds and the TAM): one close, comprising just three roods or 0.3ha, was until recently in joint ownership.

Towns Field represents another compartment within the common arable field. The boundary between it and West Field is marked by an irregular wall (Group 3) and a line of ash trees. The alignment of field boundaries also changes, Towns Field being characterised by long, narrow walled enclosures, each of a few acres and running north/south; several were in joint ownership, as shown on the TAM. One close is named New Field and another, New Dyke (TAM). The latter is described as being bounded to the west by 'the Ringe fence', a reference to the boundary of the primary enclosure (1756).[42] The presence of trees and thorns in field boundaries suggests relatively early partitioning by hedges, later replaced by walls. Walls are generally classified as irregular (Group 3) although, in comparison with the West Field, field boundaries and land ownerships are more labile. References in a later deed (1768) to Great Flatts (presumably Flatts on the TAM) as 'lately enclosed', and to 'the Long Flatts in Hebden Town Field' confirm that consolidation and enclosure continued into the second half of the eighteenth century.[43]

A close named Overends, among those listed in 1693 and one of several (re)named Overlands on the TAM, lies to the north of the B6265 and 'up slope' from strips in the common field. A mis-match between field boundaries lying on either side of the road suggests that the line of the turnpike follows an old boundary, headland or access road that preceded enclosure of the open field(s). This point is reinforced by the occurence of roadside trees and thorns and the existence of holloways on the approach to Isingdale Beck (Fig 2). Taken together, these observations suggest that the turnpike, and later the modern road, followed the line of what was already a favoured 'short cut' to Grassington.

Owners of houses at the north end of the nuclear village, both within and outside the toft compartment, and in the peripheral hamlet of Garnshaw, held land in Towns Field and Overlands (TAM). However, it is also clear that by mid-century land redistribution was in progress, some holdings having expanded at the expense of others (eg

---

[39] eg WYCRO - RD: G 500/615 (1714); AW 152/184 (1761).
[40] WYCRO - RD: AM 131/175 (1756).
[41] WYCRO - RD: AW 152/184 (1761).
[42] WYCRO - RD: AM 131/175 (1756).
[43] WYCRO - RD: BI 101/139 (1768).

Town Head Farm; see below).

Overall, these observations support the thesis that the general process of enclosure proceeded piecemeal and slowly, with open field agriculture continuing through the eighteenth century and lasting for more than 150 years after ownership of the manor passed to freeholders. However, indications of hedged boundaries suggest that enclosure in Towns Field began before that in the West Field, while the securing of 'Cross Thornes' probably took place first: ie in the pre- or early post-Conquest period.

4.3.3. Town Head hamlet and the NW and NE primary enclosures

(Figs 26, 27, 36-39, 40-42)

As already indicated, we categorise Hebden as a partly planned village, with Town Hill and Brook Street forming an irregular settlement, adjacent to the planned toft compartment but delimited by the old east/ west route through the village. Land in and around the NW and NE primary enclosures has generally been attached to dwellings in Town Head hamlet. Unfortunately we lack information about forms of tenure and do not know whether there were differences in the status of occupants within, and outside, Hebden manor. There are hints from more recent times, however, that inhabitants of Town Head hamlet traditionally had a less regulated existence than those in the manorial toft compartment. For example, the hamlet seems to have been a focus for home-based craft activities, such as textile manufacture. And, as judged by numbers of eighteenth century title deeds, changes in ownership seem to have taken place more often than occurred within the toft compartment. However, it remains possible that - at some time - the hamlet was incorporated into a 'unitary authority', with land in the northern primary enclosures augmenting that available in the southern sector of the village and managed as outfield, for the benefit of the community as a whole (Overton 1996, 22-35).

Buildings within the hamlet include a substantial early seventeenth century farmhouse and barn at Town Head and two houses of the same period in Brook Street. One of the latter has a late seventeenth century addition with an elaborate interior plaster frieze, indicative of high status; decoration of this type is rare in Craven (YVBSG 1999, 12-21, 32-34, 35; Harrison and Hutton 1984, 195). A situation at the upper end of settlements, beside stock routes, are features shared with similarly-named hamlets elsewhere in north-west England (M. Atkin, *pers comm*). Occupiers of the three major houses in Hebden's Town Head hamlet would have been well-positioned to monitor the passage of animals and other traffic through and within the township, *ie* via the east/west route, or along High Green to Hebden Moor.

A field named Tofts lies inside the NW primary enclosure, to the north of Town Head barn (TAM). It contains earthworks, some representing ridge and furrow and oth-

ers possibly the remains of house platforms. Today the western field boundary of Tofts is formed by a wall classified as irregular (Group 3). It lies along an obvious embankment and is shown on the first edition 6in OS map (1857) as heavily treed. The northern boundary of the enclosure overlies an earthwork in the form of a mound, approximately 100m in diameter and slightly domed (Figs 52, 53). It appears to be at least partly artificial *(ie* shaped by levelling the end of a natural spur).[44] Its significance and likely period is implied by the name Sedber. This first appears in the deed of 1598 as a named enclosure containing a particular 'pcell of meadowe'; it also relates to three fields adjacent to Tofts and appearing on the TAM. The mound may represent a township meeting place, of the type described by Moorhouse (2003, 303).

Margaret Gelling (*pers comm*) comments as follows:

'Sedber is one of several instances of a compound place-name *set-berg*, which is of Old Norse origin. The literal meaning is 'seat hill' and the usual interpretation is 'flat-topped hill'. No striking natural feature deserving this term has been noted at the town called Sedbergh, or at the other places (Sedbury in the North Riding, Sedberge in County Durham) which are of identical or analogous origin, and it is possible that the clear association of the term with an artificial mound in Hebden provides a clue to the significance of the compound place-name. This would be a suitable term for a mound used (and perhaps constructed) for administrative and judicial assemblies.'

One of three common fields in neighbouring Grassington carries the same name, first recorded in 1603. No earthwork has been found; however, much of this erstwhile common field has been subject to land-development (Jean Booth, *pers comm*).[45] Although the Hebden example has only recently been recognised, its existence - together with other earthworks in the field named Tofts - is consistent with our view that a settlement site at the northern end of today's village preceded the planned toft compartment, an inference confirmed by Moorhouse (2003, 306).

Landholdings within the NW primary enclosure are orientated east/west, running 'up slope' (TAM); irregular walls (Group 3) form ownership boundaries and most field divisions. However, the existence of a boulder wall and treed boundary - running with the contour, cut by ownership boundaries and most obvious where it divides Low Field and Great Field - suggests an earlier division between the higher pastures and more productive lower ground: it may represent a head-dyke, comparable to that found in the SE primary enclosure (see above). Cultivation terraces, boulder walls and treed boundaries - features considered indicative of early settlement - are also to be found lying between Hole Bottom Farm and High Garnshaw. During the 1730s these lands were shared by four holdings, but by 1846/7 (TAM) most had been acquired by Hole Bottom Farm, with a few attached to Hole Bottom Cottage (Joy 1991, 19-26). Hole Bottom hamlet is situated beside the entry to the raikes and just outside the perim-

---

[44] GPS survey by I Dormer, Historic Landscape Management Consultant and field visit by K. Cale, Community Archaeologist. Their assistance is greatly appreciated.

[45] Observations by Mrs Jean Booth with other members of the Upper Wharfedale Field Society, whose collaboration is much appreciated.

eter of the primary enclosure (Fig 45); the farm holds land both within and outside the latter.

The largest landholding in the north-west quadrant, second only to Ranelands within the township, is that attached to Town Head Farm. Its acreage was increased during the latter part of the eighteenth century by purchase (YVBSG 1999,12-15, 32-34), (Fig 38). Neighbouring Pickering End Farm was bought in 1721 as part of an endowment made by Richard Fountaine for his hospital (alms houses) in the nearby township of Linton;[46] the farmhouse dates from this period.

The fourth of the primary enclosures lies in the NE quadrant. Its boundary, limited by the terrain, encompasses the whole of an albeit small area suitable for cultivation, including a close named Corn Field (described as arable and meadow, TAM; Figs 42, 51). Boulder walls predominate both within and outside this primary enclosure, wall-structure apparently reflecting the nature and availability of stone, rather than uniformly early dates of construction. Walls inside the primary enclosure overlie the remains of lynchets and boundaries (probably hedged) that have gone out of use. The ownership of closes inside this enclosure named 'Nows' (or Knowles Land) relate to a house in Town Head hamlet (Fig 54), occupied by Henry Ibbotson whose name appears on a list of Hebden landholders from 1673.[47] Subsequently Knowles land formed the endowment of a local charity, established in 1723 by Robert Ibbotson with the object of supporting apprentices and assisting the poor of the parish; it subsequently funded the building of the village institute (1903).

4.3.4. Peripheral settlements
(Fig 43)

Fields created inside the four primary enclosures generally relate to farms within the nuclear village while closes attached to small settlements (hamlets, farms, and cottage holdings), dispersed on the periphery of the SE, NE and NW primary enclosures, complete the patchwork of fields lying between nuclear village and moor. Seventeen such holdings can be defined. They divide into the long- and short-lived, the latter now derelict.

Garnshaw farm occupies the western sector of the township, outside the NW primary enclosure. High Garnshaw farm and Hole Bottom hamlet similarly lie just outside the ring fence. Until Hebden's stinted pasture was enclosed (c 1600) intercommoned land associated with Garnshaw hamlet straddled the present Hebden/Grassington boundary and extended westwards to Isingdale beck, the line of

the medieval boundary (Beaumont et al 2004, 75, Fig 7.5). Fields associated with High Garnshaw represent intakes from Hebden Moor. Some of them lie outside a handful of small closes 'tacked on' to the western perimeter wall of the NW primary enclosure. Held by Brow House in the 1730s, the latter were subsequently absorbed into Hole Bottom farm (Fig 38). Again, the classification of wall types and wall abutments clearly shows the sequence in which walls were established, and those that subsequently went out of use.

Outside the eastern boundary of the NE primary enclosure, Scar Top and Copper Gill may represent early settlements or staging posts on the east-west route. They developed as self-contained holdings, each within its own oval enclosure. On the steep rocky slopes around Scar Top and Scarside there is a collection of small irregular closes or crofts, bounded by boulder walls - some of the boulders very large indeed. Particular features of the NE quadrant, this area merits further investigation, particularly in view of the proximity of two Bronze Age burial mounds on moorland to the east of Scar Top house (Raistrick 1964). Alternatively, all or some of the small walled enclosures may represent intakes made, or utilised, by the occupants of small 'squatter settlements' on the edge of the moor. During the late eighteenth and early nineteenth centuries, dwellings lying outside the perimeter boundaries of the primary enclosures were home to 'incomers', drawn to the area by the prospect of employment in an active lead industry in Grassington and the potential for similar opportunities in Hebden. These homes were abandoned when, with the advent of parliamentary enclosure and the allocation of allotments to major landowners, access (licit or illicit) to grazing and other resources from the moorland commons was terminated.

As well as illustrating those peripheral landholdings that survived up to the time of the TAM, our map (Fig 43) also shows enclosures held by the township and still administered by the civil parish. This land borders routeways, specifically: (1) the drove route that ran along High Green and (ii), the modern road where it approaches the village from the east, following the course of the turnpike. References to the farm known as Wygill (why, a heifer) enter the documented history in 1670 and it seems likely that its site moved from that now occupied by Edge House, sometime after construction of the turnpike. Farm buildings of the latter-day Wygill lie over and amongst the remains of holloways on Hebden Bank and the newly-created enclosures that fringed the turnpike (Figs 28, 31).

---

[46] WYCRO - RD: CC 160/224 (1730).
[47] Valuation of estates and land in Hebden, 1673. MS no. RS1011.1; Raistrick collection, Ironbridge museum, Shropshire.

Part 5: Landscape and community

The activities of many generations have left their mark on the Hebden landscape and/or in the written record. In this review of significant phases in the development of the village and township, periods of change in the physical environment are related to coeval social structures and the nature and sequence of occupation and landownership.

5.1. Territory and settlement

Mans' presence in and around Hebden during prehistoric times is deduced from the archaeological record, preserved in the landscape (see Part 2.l). However, we do not know when the likely transition from periodic migration to permanent occupation took place, nor can we define the location or nature of early settlement (*ie* whether focal, dispersed, or a mix - as suggested by the present pattern of centrally- and peripherally-placed habitations). Factors favouring settlement and influencing location include the existence of through routes and beck- and river-crossings (Beaumont *et al* 2003) as well as the opportunities afforded by the terrain and the availability of natural resources.

Another unknown is the period when the territory of the township was defined and its perimeter boundary established; the possibility that some boundary markers date from the Bronze Age is considered elsewhere (Beaumont *et al* 2004, 77). Indications of settlement in the locality during the pre-Conquest period derive from the status of Burnsall as the centre of an Anglo-Saxon estate and parish, and from its collection of stone sculptures: Viking hogback grave markers are indicative of a secular community of high status. Norse influence in Hebden is implied by the field-name Sedber and the earthwork to which it refers (see Introduction and Part 4.3.3). Archaeological study is required to confirm and date this mound and other earthworks in the field named Tofts: the results may show whether the area designated as Town Head hamlet represents a settlement site that preceded the planned section of the village.

5.2. Planned landscapes: lords and peasants

Preliminary stages in the formation of Hebden's planned landscape cannot   be defined or dated at present, although it is generally accepted that the formation of primary enclosures took place at an early stage in the development of settlement, foreshadowing a period of communally-managed, open field cultivation (Lewis *et al* 2001, 191-2; Roberts and Wrathmell 2002, 116-17). The outcome of our survey of field boundaries, and comparison with the work of other investigators, suggests that oval enclosures originated during the medieval period, but could be older (see Part 1.4).   In this context, our finding of Group 1 boundaries between arable and pasture in the SE and NW primary enclosures seems to signal a precursor stage, with the development of definitive 'ovals' resulting from subsequent expansion to include good quality pasture. The position of Hebden on a trans-Pennine

routeway must have provided an incentive to establish, enlarge and/or maintain the four primary enclosures (as described in this study), particularly after Fountains Abbey had been granted rights of passage through the manor lands (see Part 2). However, this does not preclude the possibility that stock-proof barriers were created in response to other or earlier influences: the double oval enclosure at Roystone Grange is securely dated to the Romano-British period (Hodges 1991; Wildgoose 1991). Further studies of Hebden may reveal earlier elements, encapsulated within the landscape that we know today.

In northern England the genesis of nucleated villages, characteristically regular in form, generally took place between the late eleventh and thirteenth centuries (Roberts 1990, 109): an in-depth consideration of the theory and practice of dating villages is provided by the same author (1992). Planned components within Hebden exhibit features considered typical, notably the grouping of six to twelve tofts or house plots to form a rectangular toft compartment, topographically associated with a common arable field and intervening back lane (see Part 3.2). At the same time, single farmsteads or small hamlets were usually situated on the periphery of primary enclosures, along circumferential trackways and with access to outer pastures (*eg* Hole Bottom; see Part 2.1). (For a review of case-studies and landscapes of enclosure, see Roberts and Wrathmell 2002, 94-103, 116-17, 147-55.)

Features described above epitomise a distinct phase of settlement organisation or reorganisation, often linked with post-Conquest developments in feudalism. The upshot was the establishment of highly-organised communities and countryside, with control depending upon a balance between lords (or their agents) and the manor courts. As well as the initiation and management of open-field agriculture characterised by strip holdings, their collective responsibilities included the control of pasture rights and access to natural resources (Lewis *et al* 2001).

Poll Tax returns provide a glimpse of the community in medieval Hebden.[48] In 1377 payment by 45 individuals is recorded. This compares with 23 in 1379 (when evasion was rife). The latter shows that the highest sums were paid by three craftsmen, *ie* cooper and fuller (vj.d = six old pence), and dyer (xij.d, twelve pence). The rest paid the minimum of four pence (iiij), the standard rate for the peasantry and indicative of a farming community under manorial control. The population of Grassington was similarly constituted. In contrast, almost a third of those listed in Appletreewick can be classified as craftsmen (*eg* smith, shoemaker, carpenter, butcher, and four tailors), all paying six old pence. At that time Appletreewick manor was amongst the possessions of Bolton Priory and its community probably provided a ready market for the artisans, with further opportunities for trade at Appletreewick's annual autumn fair.

Of Hebden's lords, three names emerge from the known

---

[48] (i) Public Record Office (Kew), E179/206/34, *Poll Tax, 1377.* (ii) YAS MS from Miss L.M. Midgley's Transcripts, 1397. (iii) The Returns for the West Riding of the County of York of the Poll Tax (AD 1379), *(1882). Yorks Archaeol J.* **7**, 265-6.

biographical details as the most likely to have been responsible for establishing a planned nuclear village. The first is Osbern de Arches. In 1086 he held some sixty manors in the Vale of York, of which 95% have village plans classified as regular or partly regular (Sheppard 1976). Hebden is one of three manors that he held in the Pennines, those at Silsden and Burnsall similarly showing traces of a single row toft compartment (Crossley and Hill 1993, 4-5; Dalton 1994, 58-60). Thus the rudiments of a late eleventh century village plan may survive in today's Hebden, possibly underlying the product of a subsequent reorganisation that reflected the aspirations and fortunes of a later manorial lord. For example, around 1240 Nicholas de Hebden added a regularly-planned row of tofts on his newly-acquired manor of Eske (Holderness, East Yorkshire), (English and Miller 1991): he may have similarly improved his holdings in Wharfedale. Alternatively, his grandson Sir William de Hebden (c 1264-1325) might have been responsible. As a follower of Robert Clifford (1st Lord of the Honour of Skipton), guardian of his heirs and protector of Skipton castle, he had high status and strong local ties. In 1315/16 he was granted free warren in the demesne lands of his Wharfedale manors (Hebden, Burnsall, Conistone) and also at Eske (Clay 1947).

5.3. Enclosure

The operation of open field agriculture and dispersion of individual landholdings is confirmed in the deed of 1598, *ie* nine years after the acquisition of the manor by freeholders (see Part 4.1.). Enclosure is considered by Williamson (2000, 56) to be 'one of the most important processes to have shaped the English cultural landscape'. The phased and prolonged nature of enclosure in the Hebden landscape is demonstrated by our classification and mapping of field boundaries. This survey also enabled us to define compartments within and outside the nuclear village and to produce a model of the manorial landscape (see Part 3).

Fundamental changes, initiated by freeholders, fitted the pattern of large-scale and widespread redistribution of land that began with the dissemination of monastic holdings after the Dissolution. An early development (c 1600) was the designation and enclosure of a large stinted pasture on Hebden Moor (see Part 4.2). Again this was consistent with contemporary custom, extending the area of grazing that could be controlled more closely than that on the open moor, or in areas of intercommoning between townships (Winchester 2000, 78).

Coterminosity between sections of the boundary of the stinted pasture and the township boundary suggests that they were established simultaneously. Action by Hebden freeholders may have been precipitated by the need to defend their interests against those of a more powerful neighbour, Grassington. Between 1597 and 1605 Grassington tenants were beset by demands from their manorial lord, George Clifford, third Earl of Cumberland, courtier and privateer, who was engaged in raising funds to meet his considerable debts (Spence 1995, 191-206). Hence Hebden freeholders may have elected to protect their assets and 'draw the line' in the form of a marked boundary wall.

The advent of multiple ownership stimulated the rationalisation of landholdings, with the consolidation of strips

in the open fields by sale or exchange and the establishment of field boundaries - the process known as piecemeal enclosure (Williamson 2003a, 16-17). In Hebden, piecemeal enclosure, or enclosure by agreement, apparently involved the redistribution of strips of arable and meadow and the subdivision of pasture lying within the oval enclosures (see Part 4.3). As well as contributing to the limits of primary enclosures, boundaries incorporating trees, thorn bushes, boulders and/or orthostats (Group 1) also occur in some property- and field-boundaries, where there is also evidence of arable cultivation (see Parts 1 and 4). These boundaries probably represent a phase of piecemeal enclosure, dating from the manorial or early post-manorial period(s). Walls which we have classified as irregular (Group 3) form property boundaries and numerous field divisions; they characterise closes dated from title deeds to between the mid- seventeenth and later eighteenth century. The few walls classified as regular (Group 4) represent the most recent generation of field divisions. Intakes from the peripheral moorland, enclosed by a variety of walling types, additionally contribute to the area of piecemeal enclosure. Fortuitously the TAM was compiled at a time when piecemeal enclosure was almost complete (1846/7). Comparative mapping has shown that some field boundaries have subsequently been adjusted or gone out of use - a trend that continues - gradually, rather than dramatically.

Field divisions inside the primary enclosures enter the written record in the late seventeenth century and the process continued for around 200 years probably reaching a peak in the middle decades of the eighteenth century. Piecemeal enclosure on the manor of Askwith in mid-Wharfedale occupied a similar period, although documentary evidence showed that 'most strip aggregations were fenced with walls, trees or hedges' by1596 (Pickles and Bosworth 1991). In Hebden, the protracted nature of piecemeal enclosure must surely relate to the necessity for negotiation and agreement involving around fifty freeholders (see below). In contrast, parliamentary or general enclosure (1857) was imposed 'from above' and benefited the best-endowed landholders in the community; thirty-six were awarded allotments which, walled within eighteen months, brought about the wholesale remodelling of the stinted pasture and moorland commons.

Land-use also related to changes in the pattern of farming, linked with an expanding and improved transport system. In mid-nineteenth century Hebden there were only 30a (12ha) of arable in the township as a whole, compared with 350a (142ha) of meadow, 518a (210ha) of pasture and 2,650a (1072ha) of moor (TAM). Even the most favoured areas in the township are marginal for cultivation and are assumed to have been converted to grass once grain, flour and other commodities could be bought in: from 1777 there was access to the Leeds-Liverpool canal at Gargrave, some 14km distant (Wright 1985, 120, 175-80).

5.4. Buildings and community; industrial interlude

Major phases of house building paralleled the process of field enclosure and drystone walling. During the late seventeenth and eighteenth centuries buildings with thatched roofs supported by wooden crucks were rebuilt in stone. As already noted, principal houses in the toft compartment have features typical of the vernacular style of the later seventeenth century. These changes took place during a period of agricultural prosperity in Craven - a consequence of general improvements in the management of livestock, particularly cattle (Harrison and Hutton 1984, 224-31; Winchester 2000, 146-48).

During the period of major rebuilding the number of households in Hebden showed a modest increase. Thirty-seven houses were listed in the Hearth Tax returns for Hebden (1672), although manifestations of prosperity were decidedly low key: twenty-six of the houses had just one hearth, and none had more than two. A valuation of land and estates, compiled a year later, listed 50 holdings and the names of 56 owners and occupiers 'resident or not' in the township.[49] Almost a century later the first land tax assessment (1760) recorded forty-seven owners - and fifty in 1782, when owners and occupiers were listed separately for the first time. Deeds of title show a large number of transactions through the eighteenth century, with holdings sold or mortgaged by local yeomen to non-residents - typically town and city 'gentlemen' or major landowners. For example, Green House farm was mortgaged to Thomas and Ayscough Fawkes of Farnley, Esquires (1750 and 1755). Later Thomas Chamberlain, landowner and agriculturalist of Skipton, foreclosed on a mortgage on Ranelands held by 'wheeler-dealer' Richard Constantine. Vendors included the sons of Hebden yeomen who sold their inheritances, having moved away and 'made good'. They included Peter Brown, cornfactor, York (1768); James Topham, jeweller, London (1782) and Thomas Topham, bellmonger, Chester (1783). Purchasers included John Hawkridge of Grassington and Pateley Bridge, apothecary and surgeon (Lone House; 1759 and 1766) and Mr William Skelton of Leeds, gentleman (Town Head, 1760-1803). The latter increased the size of his holding by purchase, also acquiring land in neighbouring townships. Similarly, members of the Chamberlain family consolidated their landholding at Ranelands, a process completed during the first decade of the nineteenth century. By the time of the tithe survey (1846/7), although the number of landholders remained little changed (ie at forty-eight), only one farm (Saxelby; Fig 34) was owner-occupied. It seems likely that many purchases of property, including small portions of unattached land, were speculative ventures encouraged, not only by the increased profitability of agriculture, but also by the possibility of freeholders' royalties from lead. Although the Hebden Moor Mining Company did not get under way until 1856, hopes for the future must have been encouraged by the precedent of a long-established enterprise on Grassington Moor (Gill 1993).

A period of water-powered industrial activity (textiles and lead extraction) reached a peak during the middle years of the nineteenth century in both Hebden and Grassington. In general, those involved in the capitalisation of these ventures were non-residents. However, the new developments brought an influx of labour and rise in population. Houses in Hebden were divided to accommodate more families and there were some additions to the housing stock. Although smaller in scale, this expansion has features in common with the 'late nucleation' and creation of

polyfocal villages, linked with industrialisation, which took place in nearby mid-Nidderdale (Muir 1998, 75). In Hebden new cottages appeared on the mill site and in Brook Street (TAM) and the population rose between 1801 and 1831 (from 341 to 435) then declined - at first gradually and then rapidly - to a low in 1901 of 199. These changes were brought about principally by the movement of industrial workers.[50]

Over the same period the numbers occupied in Hebden's core activity, agriculture, were less affected. Heads of farming households remained more-or-less constant, at twenty-one to twenty-four, between 1841 and 1891, although the number of individuals in farming households fell by about 30% in later decades, chiefly through a reduction in house- and farm-servants. Thus Hebden did not entirely escape the effects of the agricultural depression of the 1870s, although the upland tradition of pastoral agriculture managed on family-run farms fostered stability.

While Hebden's Back Lane survives and the planned toft compartment is not difficult to recognise, the layout and appearance of the village altered considerably during the eighteenth and nineteenth centuries, after the east/west route had been turnpiked and realigned. The TAM shows that some infill building had taken place in the most northerly tofts, obscuring earlier property boundaries. An unflattering description of the village in the first decades of the nineteenth century is provided by Speight (1988, 455). Writing in 1900, he describes Hebden as 'a very primitive looking place'. He refers to those who remember 'the tottering bridge in the Beck bottom' (ie the turnpike bridge) and 'several old unplastered cottages, with thatched roofs and rough cobble walls'. The school was said to be 'more like a common mistal than a place of intellectual light'.

Primitive Methodist and Wesleyan chapels (the former now demolished), the church (chapel-of-ease, Linton parish) and public house were nineteenth century additions to the toft compartment (Figs 26, 27, 55, 56). A new school was built in 1875 to replaced the premises, justly alluded to above, housed in the corn-drying kiln! (Evidence of its original function is provided by an eye-witness account of its demolition; Bland c 1875, 19-20.) Main Street replaced the unwalled access road between Kiln Green and the eastern boundaries of the tofts; Green Terrace appeared in 1877, facing east onto Main Street and including premises for a post office. Many seventeenth century houses were refenestrated: this involved the enlargement of windows, with the wholesale replacement of mullions by square-cut jambs and lintels. Together with the survival of a relatively large number of cottage dwellings, these architectural features confer a nineteenth century appearance and uniformity throughout the village that belies its earlier origins (YVBSG 1999, 5-6). Building developments followed hard on the heels of a period of prosperity, when eligible freeholders shared mining royalties to the sum of £3,345 (modern equivalent £155,000; Joy et al 2002, 64-70). The extent to which these profits benefitted the community as a whole cannot be quantified, although a local inhabitant, writing in 1927 at the age of 82, refers to great changes in Hebden between 1850 and 1870, undertaken 'out of pride for the village'.

[49] see **fn 47**.
[50] see **fn 32**.

APPENDICES

Appendix 1
See Figures 28 and 29: perimeter boundary of SE primary enclosure, numbered (1) - (7)

Largest of the four enclosures (c.1.0 x 1.0km), much of its western boundary follows the 'lip' of Hebden Gill (1) marked by stretches of relic hedgerow and tumbled walling. Its south-western and southern limits lie along a bluff above the river Wharfe (2) running parallel to the township boundary (centre stream), then following Skuff Beck (3), with stretches of wall (Group 1) and hedgerow, up to Hartlington Raikes Road (4) and a well-marked bank and ditch flanked (to the east) by an irregular (Group 3) wall (5). The northern boundary is represented partly by a small ditch and a bank topped by a few hawthorns (6) and partly by substantial walling (Group 3), also on a low bank (7).

Appendix 2
See Figures 32 and 33: perimeter boundary of SW primary enclosure, numbered (1) - (7)

Area c. 0.5 x 0.75 km, cut by the B6265 Pateley Bridge to Grassington Road. To the north a relic hedgerow comprising a line of aged hawthorns, tumbled walling and a bank and ditch (1), then a section of intact walling (Group 3),(2)..The western section, coterminous with the township boundary, is marked by a watercourse (New Dyke (3) which becomes Howgill Beck (4)); here the boundary is secured by walls on the Grassington side of the watercourse. To the south a stretch of rebuilt wall (Group 4) tops a steep embankment above the river (5); the position of earlier foundations is suggested by an alignment of around 10 large boulders, most of them free-standing. Towards the village the boundary follows Lythe Flatt Lane and Back Lane (6,7).

Appendix 3
See Figures 36 and 37: perimeter boundary of NW primary enclosure, numbered (1) - (5)

A well-defined boundary, enclosing an area of c.1.0 x 0.5 km. A wall with orthostats and recumbent boulders forms the boundary with High Green (1); it has unilaterally protruding through stones on the side of the droveway. A second droving funnel passes east/west between the curved south-western boundary of this enclosure ((2); Group 3 wall) and that of the SW primary enclosure. From Pickering End farm northwards the boundary of the NW enclosure is marked by a robust wall incorporating orthostats and boulders which runs along an embankment and parallels the township boundary (3). A finger of moorland extends between the two boundaries; it has been encroached upon by the formation of intakes and an enclosure close (EAM). Two further intakes relate to the northern boundary of the primary enclosure, helping to create a droving funnel along Hebden Raikes (4); a second funnel is bordered by an Enclosure wall. Access to the village passes to the west of Hole Bottom hamlet (5) and via High Green.

Appendix 4
See figures 40 and 41: perimeter boundary of NE primary enclosure, numbered (1) - (5)

The smallest of the primary enclosures (c. 0.5 x 0.25 km) and on a steep, south-west facing slope. Much of its upper, eastern boundary is marked by an impressive wall incorporating random boulders - some huge (ie having dimensions > 1.5m or 5ft - and roughly hewn, quarried stone, lying along a break of slope between meadowland and the steep heights of Scarside and the township quarry (1). The eastern and south-eastern parts of the boundary are difficult to define (2,3) with closes apparently added to, or merged with, the primary enclosure. The south-western section of the perimeter boundary, lying just above Hebden Beck, has been largely replaced by regular (Group 4) walling (4); its earlier course can be traced along a line of wall foundations, a few aged hawthorns and mature ash trees. The northern limit of the enclosure is marked by a walled boundary that follows the contour (5).

Bibliography

Atherden, M, Bastow, M, Beaumont, H M, and Martlew, R, in prep. *A palynological study of peat deposits on the Hebden/Grassington boundary in Upper Wharfedale; ecology, archaeolological sites and human occupation.*

Atkin, M A, 1982/3 Stock Tracks Along Township Boundaries. *J English Place-Name Soc*, **15**: 24-32.

——, 1985 Some Settlement Patterns in Lancashire. In D Hooke (ed) *Medieval Villages*. Oxford: Oxford Univ Com for Archaeol, Monograph **5**: 170-85.

——, 1993 Sillfield, Preston Patrick: A double-oval type of field pattern. *Transactions of the Cumberland and Westmorland Antiquarian and Archaeological Society*, Vol **XCIII**: 145-53.

Beaumont, H M, and members of the Hebden History Group, 2003 Hebden Township, Upper Wharfedale: a case study. In R A Butlin (ed) *An Historical Atlas of North Yorkshire*. Otley: Westbury, 238-41.

——, and ——, 2004 Hebden Township Boundary, Past and Present. In R F White and P R Wilson (eds) *Ancient and Historic Landscapes of the Yorkshire Dales: Recent Work*. YAS Occ Pap No. **2**: 69-78.

Bland, J A, *c.*1875 *Hebden Sketches*. Skipton: Edmondson & Co.

Clay, C T, 1947 (ed) *Early Yorkshire Charters VII*. Yorks Archaeol Soc Extra Ser. (Wakefield), 25.

Collinson, C, 1994 The Abbot's Sheep Recalled. *Medieval Yorkshire* No. **23**: 41-46.

Crossley, M, and Hill, B, 1993 Reading between the lines of Silsden Documents. *Medieval Yorkshire No.* **22**: 2-9.

Croucher, T, 1995 *Boots and Books*. Otley: Smith Settle.

Dalton, P, 1994 *Conquest, Anarchy and Lordship: Yorkshire 1066-1154*. Cambridge Univ Press.

Edwards, W, and Trotter, F M, 1954 *British Regional Geology - The Pennines and Adjacent Areas* (3rd ed.). London: HMSO.

Ellis, A, 1875/6 Notes on Yorkshire Domesday Tenants. *Yorks Archaeol J,* **4**: 114-248, 384-415.

English, B, and Miller, K, 1991 The deserted village of Eske, East Yorkshire. *Landscape History*, **13**: 5-32.

Feather, S, 1964 Yorkshire Archaeological Register, *Yorks Archaeol J* **, 41**: 162-3.

Fleming, A, 1998 *Swaledale - Valley of the Wild River*. Edinburgh: Univ Press.

Gambles, R, 1995 *Yorkshire Dales Place-Names*. Skipton.

Gelling, M, and Cole, A, 2003 *The Landscape of Place Names*. Donington: Paul Watkins.

Greenway D E, 1972 (ed) *Charters of the Honour of Mowbray 1107-91.* Records of Social and Economic History, ns **1**.

Gill, M C, 1993 The Grassington Mines. *British Mining* No **46**.

——, 1994 The Wharfedale Mines. *British Mining* No. **49**.

Harrison B, and Hutton, B, 1984 *Vernacular Houses in North Yorkshire and Cleveland*. Edinburgh: John Donald.

Higham, M, 1988/9 Shay Names - a need for re-appraisal? *Nomina,* **12**: 89-104.

Hodge P T, 1997 Power in Hebden Gill in the mid-19th century. *British Mining* No. **59**, 148-55.

Hodges, R, 1991 *Wall-to-Wall History: The Story of Royston Grange*. London: Duckworth.

Hooke, D, 1998 Pre-Conquest woodland: its distribution and usage. *Agricultural History Reviews,* **37**:113-29.

——, D, 2000 (ed) *Landscape: the richest historical record.* Society for Landscape Studies, supplementary series **1**.

Hoskins, W G, 1955 *The Making of the English Landscape.* London: Hodder and Stoughton.

Joy, D, 1991 *Uphill to Paradise*. Hole Bottom, Hebden: private publ.

——, with members of the Hebden History Group, 2002 *Hebden-The History of a Dales Township*. Hole Bottom, Hebden: private publ.

Lancaster, W T, 1915 (ed) *Abstracts of the Charters and Other Documents Contained in the Chartulary of the Cistercian Abbey of Fountains in the West Riding of the County of York.* 2 vols. Leeds: private publ.

Lewis, C, Mitchell-Fox P, and Dyer, C, 2001 *Village Hamlet and Field. Changing Medieval Settlements in Central England.* Macclesfield: Windgather Press.

Lord, T, 2004 One on Two and Two on One: Preliminary results from a survey of drystone walls on the National Trust estate at Malham. In R F White and P R Wilson (eds) *Ancient and Historic Landscapes of the Yorkshire Dales: Recent Work.* YAS Occ Pap No. **2**: 173-186.

Moorhouse, S, 2003 The anatomy of the Yorkshire Dales: deciphering the medieval landscape. In T G Manby, S Moorhouse and P Ottaway (eds) *The Archaeology of Yorkshire - an assessment at the beginning of the 21st century.* YAS Occ Pap No. **3**: 293-362.

Muir, R, 1998 The Villages of Nidderdale. *Landscape History*, **20**: 65-82.

——, 2000 Conceptualising Landscape. *Landscapes,* **1**: 4-21

——, 2001 *Landscape Detective*. Macclesfield: Windgather.

——, 2003 The Routeways of Medieval Ripley: a case study. In R A Butlin (ed) *Historical Atlas of North Yorkshire.* Otley: Westbury, 234-38.

Overton, M*, 1996 Agricultural Revolution in England.* Cambridge: Univ Press.

Pickles, M, and Bosworth, J, 1991 Farmhold structure in a district of piecemeal enclosure: the manor of Askwith from 1596 to 1816. *Yorks Archaeol J,* **63**: 109-26.

Rackham, O, 1993 *Trees and Woodland in the British Landscape*. London: Dent.

Raistrick, A, 1933 Roman Remains and Roads in West Yorkshire. *Yorks Archaeol J* **, 31**: 214-23.

——, 1964 Yorkshire Archaeological Register, *Yorks*

Archaeol J, **41,** 325.

——, 1971 *Old Yorkshire Dales.* London: Pan.

——, 1978 *The Pennine Walls.* Clapham via Lancaster: Dalesman.

——, 1980 *Monks & Shepherds in the Yorkshire Dales.* Yorkshire Dales National Park.

Roberts, B K, 1987 *The Making of the English Village.* London: Harlow.

——, 1990 Back Lanes and Tofts, Distribution Maps and Time: Medieval Nucleated Settlement in the North of England. In *Medieval Rural Settlement in North-East England*; B E Vyner (ed). Architectural and Archaeological Society of Durham & Northumberland, Research Report No.2: 105-25.

——, 1992 Dating villages: theory and practice. *Landscape History,* **14**: 19-30.

——, and Wrathmell, S, 1998 Dispersed settlement in England: a national view. In *The Archaeology of Landscape: studies presented to Chrisopher Taylor.* P Everson and T. Williamson (eds). Manchester: Univ Press

——, ——, 2002 *Region and Place. A study of English rural settlement.* London: English Heritage.

Rowley, T, 1994 *Villages in the Landscape.* London: Dent.

Sheppard, J A, 1966 Pre-enclosure field and settlement patterns in an English Township: Wheldrake, near York. *Geografiska Annaler,* **48B**: 59-77.

——, 1976 Medieval village planning in northern England: some evidence from Yorkshire. *Journal of Historical Geography,* **2**: 3-20.

Smith, A H, 1961 *The Place Names of the West Riding of Yorkshire, Part 6.* Cambridge: English Place-Name Society **35**.

——, 1962 *The Place Names of the West Riding of Yorkshire, Part 7.* Cambridge: English Place-Name Society **36**.

Speight, H, 1900, republished 1988 *Upper Wharfedale,* Otley. Smith Settle.

Spence, R T, 1995 *The Privateering Earl.* Stroud:Alan Sutton.

Spratt, D A, 1998 Orthostatic Field Walls on the North York Moors. *Yorks Archaeol J,* **60**:149-57.

Walker, D, 1956 A site at Stump Cross, near Grassington, Yorkshire, and the Age of the Pennine Microlithic Industry. *Proc. Prehist. Soc.* **22**: 23-8.

White, R, 2002 *The Yorkshire Dales - A Landscape Through Time.* Ilkley: Great Northern Books.

——, 2003 Founders: Arthur Raistrick. *Landscapes,* **4**:111-123.

Wildgoose, M, 1991 The Drystone Walls of Roystone Grange. *Archaeol J,* **148**: 205-40.

Williamson, T, 2000 Understanding Enclosure. *Landscapes,* **1**: 56-79.

——, 2003a Understanding Fields. *The Local Historian,* **33**: 12-29.

——, 2003b *Shaping Medieval Landscapes.* Macclesfield: Windgather.

Wilson, P, 2003 The Roman Period: the first and second centuries. In R A Butlin (ed) *An Historical Atlas of North Yorkshire,* Otley: Westbury, 48-52.

Winchester, A J, 1987 *Landscape and Society in Medieval Cumbria.* Edinburgh: Univ Press.

——, 2000 *The Harvest of the Hills.* Edinburgh: Univ Press.

Wood, P N, 1996 On the little British Kingdom of Craven. *Northern Hist,* **32**: 1-20.

Wrathmell, S, 2003 Farming in Arncliffe in the 17th and 18th centuries. *Craven History,* **1**: 33-37.

Wright, G, 1985 *Roads and Trackways of the Yorkshire Dales.* Ashbourne: Moorland Publ.

Yorkshire Vernacular Buildings Study Group (YVBSG) 1999 Vernacular Buildings of Hebden. *Yorkshire Buildings,* **27**, 4-35.

Index

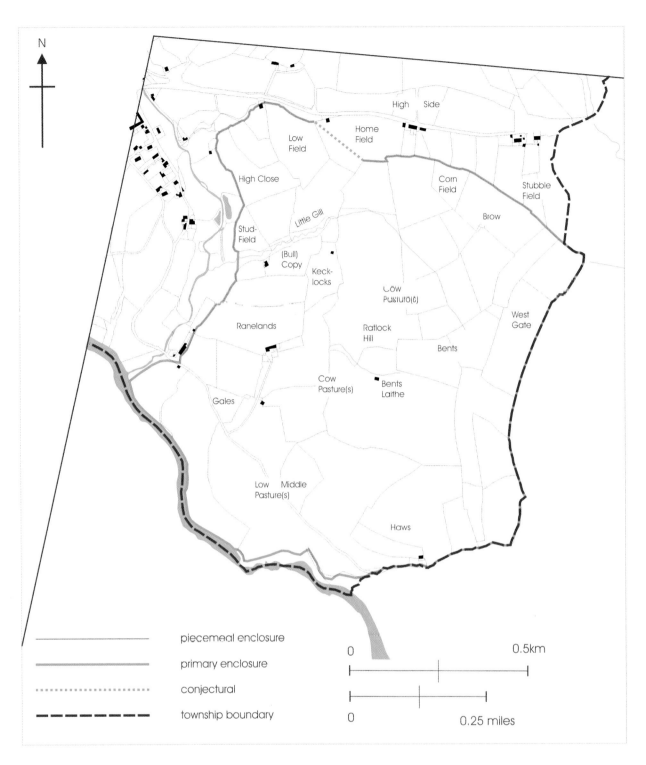

Figure 31. SE primary enclosure; field names (TAM).

Figure 32. SW primary enclosure and the line of the modern road to the west of the village where it follows the course of the turnpike, cutting across the primary enclosure. *Aerial photograph reproduced by kind permission of Ordnance Survey. © Crown Copyright. NC/04/24872.*

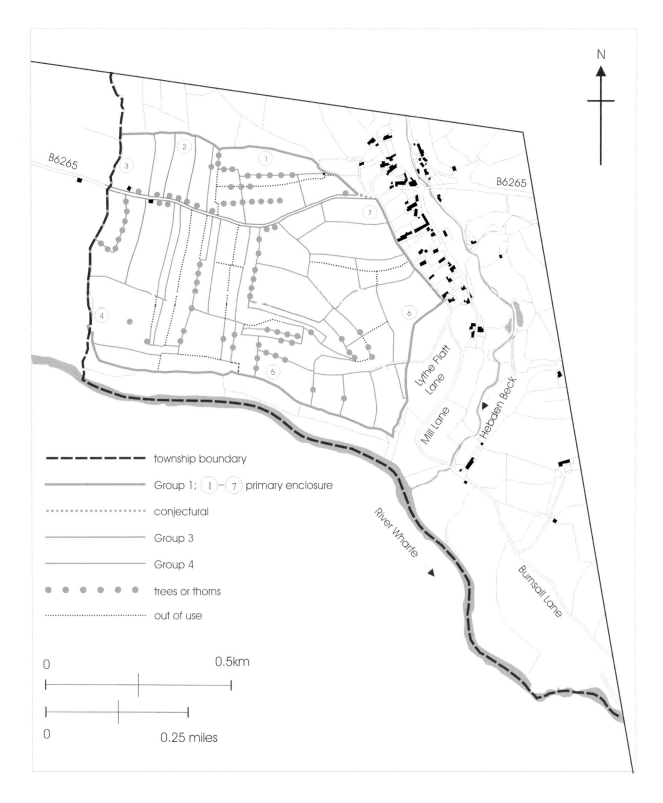

Figure 33. SW primary enclosure; outcome of field survey, including the definition and features of the perimeter boundary (see Appendix 2 for details) and classification of field boundaries.

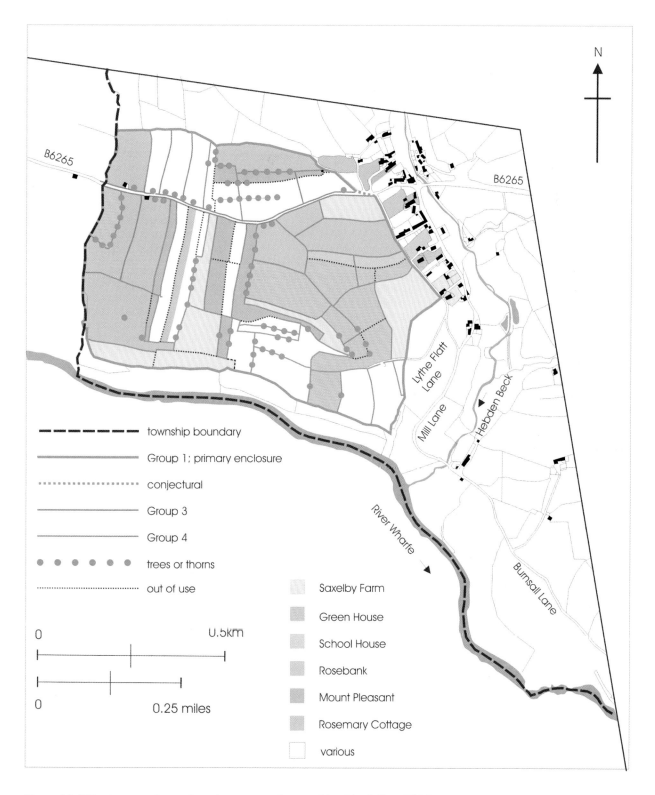

Figure 34. SW primary enclosure; boundary types and ownership of land (from TAM).

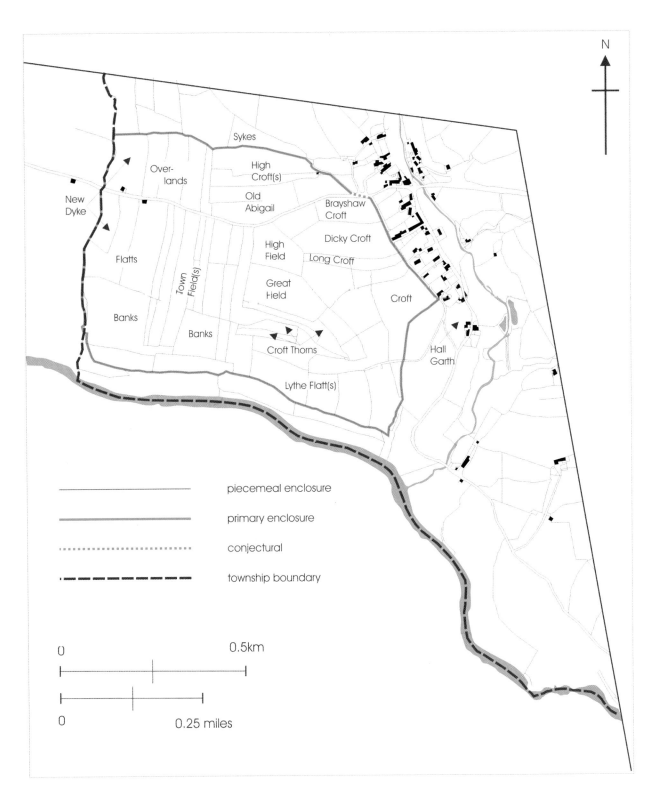

Figure 35. SW primary enclosure; field names (from TAM).

Figure 36. NW primary enclosure and part of the area known as Garnshaw. *Aerial photograph reproduced by kind permission of Ordnance Survey. © Crown Copyright. NC/04/24872.*

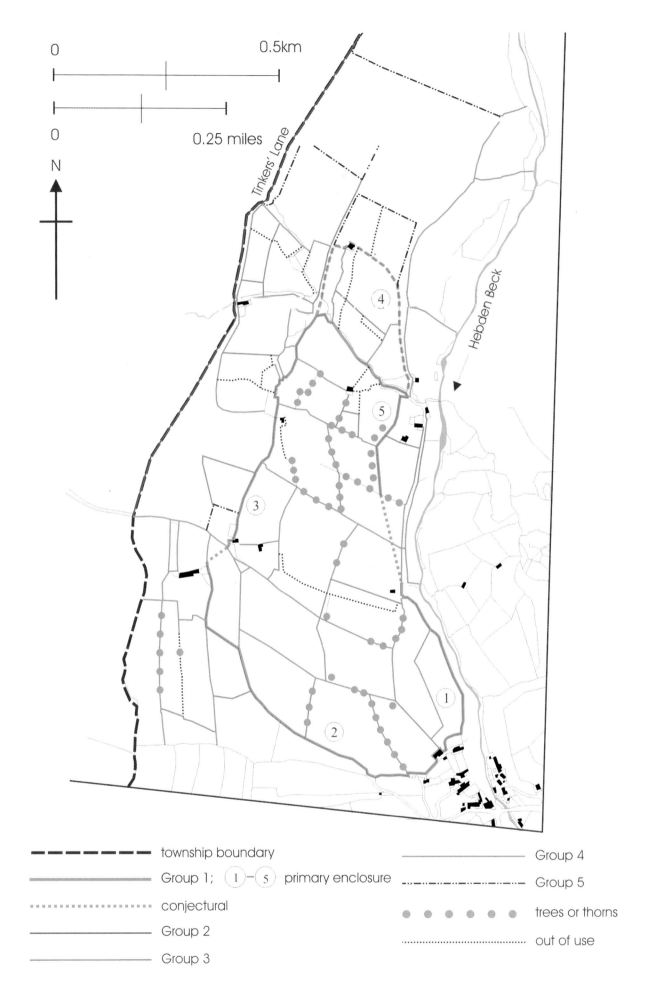

Figure 37. North-west primary enclosure, outcome of field survey: definition and features of the perimeter boundary (see Appendix 3 for details) and classification of field boundaries.

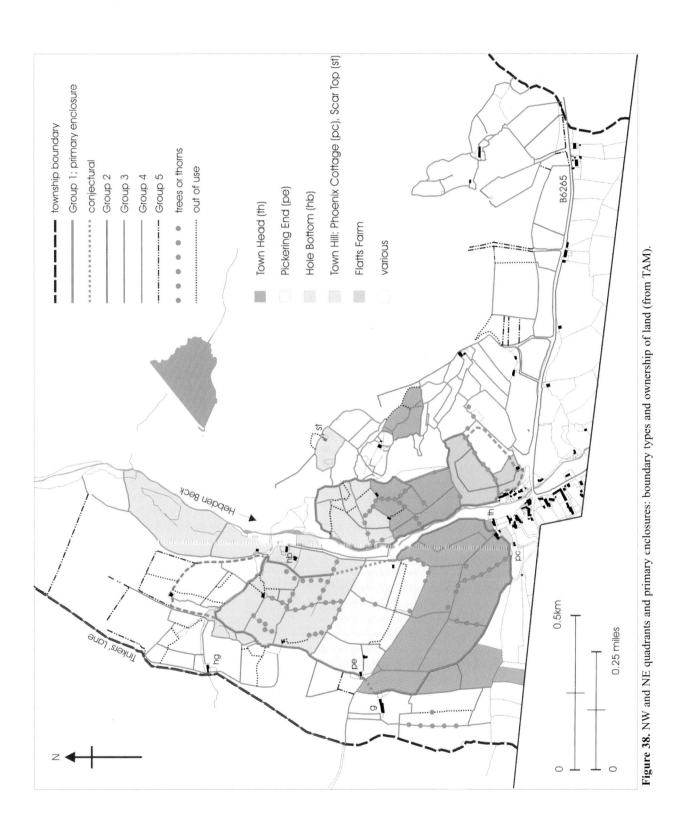

Figure 38. NW and NE quadrants and primary enclosures: boundary types and ownership of land (from TAM).

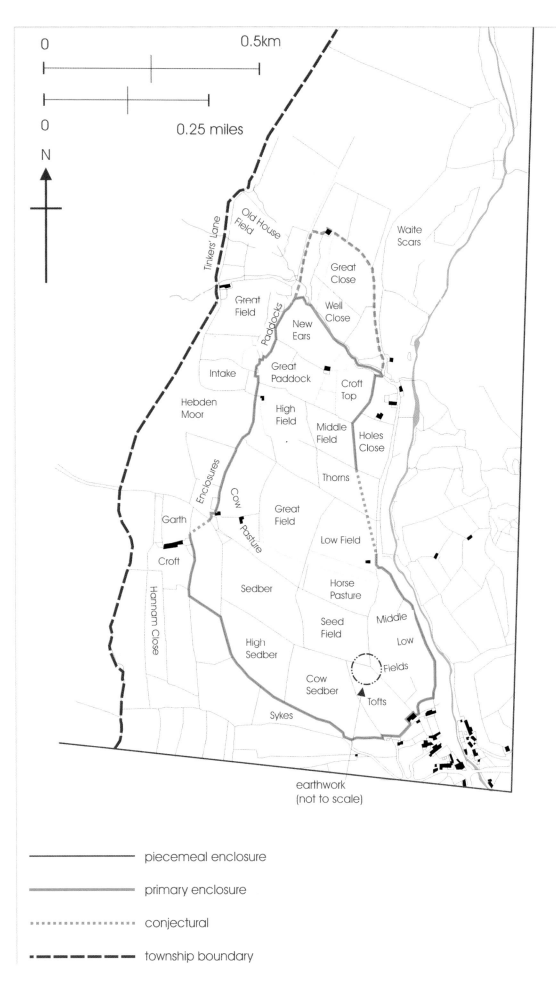

Figure 39. NW quadrant and primary enclosure: field names (from TAM).

Figure 40. NE quadrant showing areas within the primary enclosure and extending eastwards to Hebden Scar or Scarside, to heather moorland with boundaries created by the Enclosure Act; Mossy Moor reservoir appears top right. *Aerial photograph reproduced by kind permission of Ordnance Survey. © Crown Copyright. NC/04/24872.*

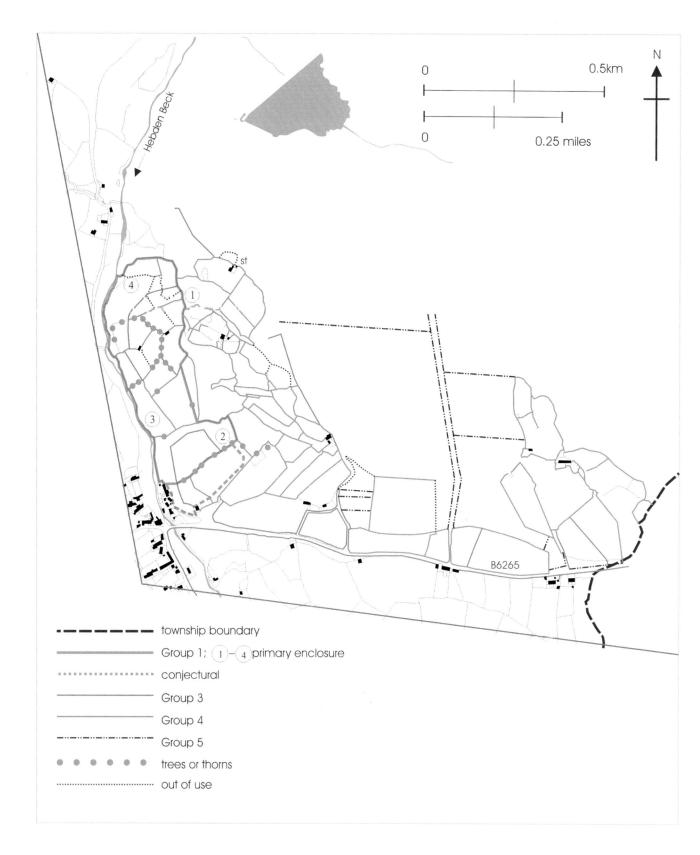

Figure 41. NE quadrant, outcome of field survey: definition and features of the perimeter boundary (see Appendix 4 for details) and classification of field boundaries.

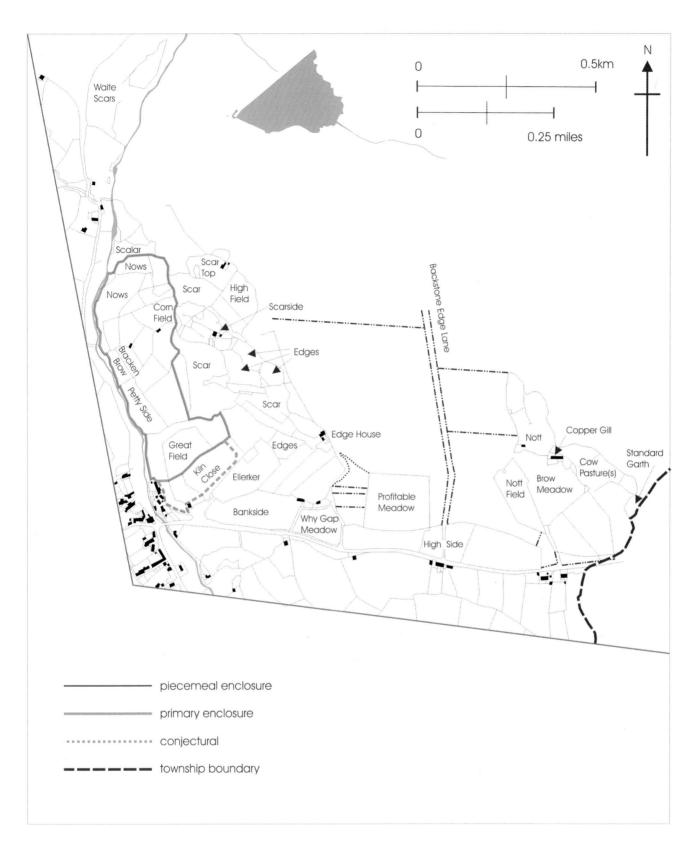

Figure 42. NE quadrant, field names (TAM).

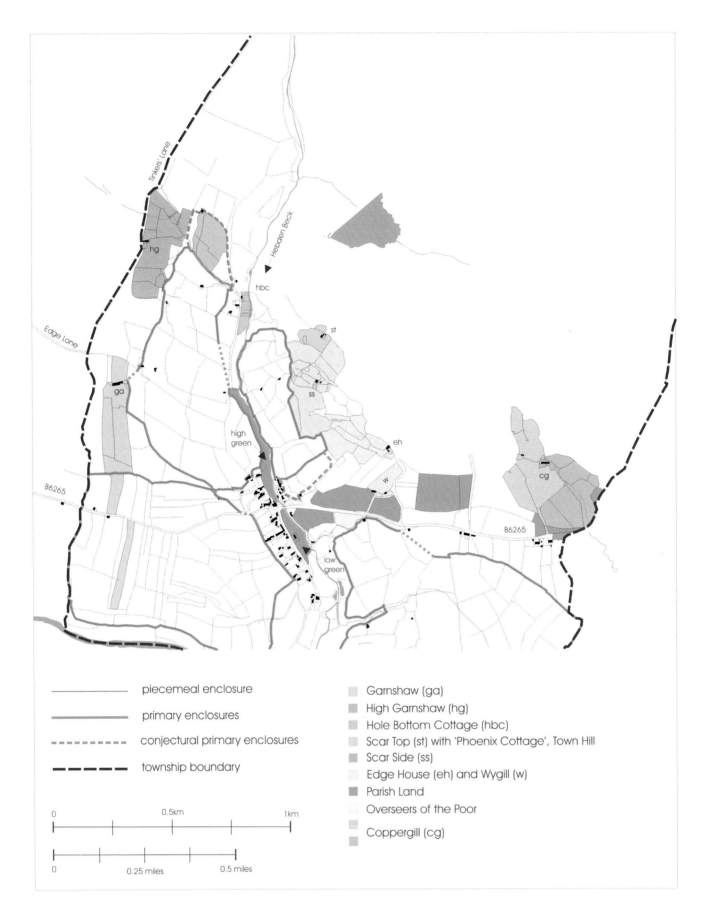

piecemeal enclosure

primary enclosures

conjectural primary enclosures

township boundary

Garnshaw (ga)
High Garnshaw (hg)
Hole Bottom Cottage (hbc)
Scar Top (st) with 'Phoenix Cottage', Town Hill
Scar Side (ss)
Edge House (eh) and Wygill (w)
Parish Land
Overseers of the Poor
Coppergill (cg)

Figure 43. Land held by farms and cottages, and by Hebden Parish, lying outside the primary enclosures.

Figure 44. River Wharfe at the confluence with Hebden Beck - the likely position of a medieval crossing point, now marked by the hippings (stepping-stones) and a footbridge built by Hebden blacksmith William Bell (1885). He re-used steel cables redundant from the lead mines.

Figure 45. Hole Bottom farm in Hebden Gill and the droveway up Hebden raikes (*ie* approaching the horizon, on the left).

Figure 46. The miners' bridge (1856); a fine example of drystone masonry, typical of the lead-mining era.

Figure 47. The 'old' Wapentake bridge (1757) and road up Town Hill. This was the route taken by traffic on the east/west route through the village, prior to construction of the turnpike: the bridge now provides access to Brook Street.

Figure 48. Ranelands farm and meadows; the land rises towards Bents Laithe and the Cow Pastures (see Figure 41).

Figure 49. West Field looking towards Back Lane and the toft compartment; thawing snow shows up the aratral curves of medieval ploughing, echoed by the reverse-S of a wall-line.

Figure 50. The bridge carrying the main road across Hebden Beck (1827); high embankments signal elevation of the road level.

Figure 51. Scar Top House appears on the horizon, with Scarside below and to the right. The wall forming the eastern boundary of the NE primary enclosure separates managed meadowland (with traces of earlier lynchets) from the boulder-strewn hillside of Hebden Scar.

Figure 52. Sedber earthwork in the field named Tofts, overlain by a field boundary and with an ash-tree marker, as seen from the south. Shallow earth banks and ridge and furrow appear in the foreground.

Figure 53. Sedber earthwork from the northwest: ridge and furrow in the field named Tofts, with Town Head barn beyond.

Figure 54. Datestone, Town Hill; probably referring to Henry Ibbotson, whose name is listed as a landholder in 1673. In 1723 the cottage was apparently occupied by Robert Ibbotson, Hebden benefactor. *Plates 52-54 published by kind permission of the Jowett family.*

Figure 55. Church of St. Peter (chapel-of-ease, Linton Parish), designed in the gothic revival style by the curate, the Rev John Feron (1841).

Figure 56. Main Street with Angle House (left) and Green Terrace, shop and post office, built in 1877. The photograph dates from the late years of the nineteenth century. *Published by kind permission of Mrs L. Wilson.*